ADVANCE PRAISE FOR

T0388986

TRANSFORMATIVE AUTOETHN
FOR PRACTITIONERS:
CHANGE PROCESSES AND PRACTICES FOR INDIVIDUALS
AND GROUPS

"What a remarkable and timely contribution to autoethnographic research! In this thoroughly researched book, the authors clear the path both theoretically and methodologically for their model of transformation as a meaningful and worthy goal of autoethnography for scholars and practitioners alike. They not only talk the talk; they walk the walk in explaining and demonstrating how transformation can be a vital part of the entire research process. This book itself is transformative in the way it lays out possibilities and processes for doing autoethnography as a change agent for ourselves as researchers, for engaging and improving the life of readers and participants in our studies, and for assisting organizations and communities to solve real-life problems. What a gift! Especially to practitioners, but also to all of us who value autoethnography for the good it can add to our world."

Carolyn S. Ellis, PhD
Distinguished Professor Emerita of Communication and Sociology
University of South Florida, USA
Recipient of Numerous Publication and Teaching Awards on Autoethnography

"Hernandez, Chang, and Bilgen—experts and leaders in collaborative autoethnography—offer a thoughtful, thorough, and easy-to-follow text that foregrounds the practical, interdisciplinary, and transformative potentials of/for doing autoethnography. Throughout, they provide astute descriptions of the autoethnographic research and writing processes, present fresh insights about working with self and others, and show how and why autoethnography is indeed "life-changing work" (p. xvii). A conversational and comprehensive book that will be of great interest to new and established autoethnographers alike."

Tony E. Adams, PhD
Caterpillar Professor and Chair of the Department of Communication
Bradley University, USA
Founding Co-editor of *The Journal of Autoethnography*

"In this engaging volume, Kathy-Ann Hernandez, Heewon Chang, and Wendy Bilgen share the transformational potential of autoethnography. This is an excellent resource for practitioners seeking to learn more about autoethnography and how to implement it to improve understanding of self, others, and society. The thoughtful process of study and change encouraged by the authors can be greatly life-enhancing. The personal stories and the models shared make the material highly accessible, an important dimension of the transformative power of the book."

Sherry Marx, PhD
Professor
School of Teacher Education and Leadership
Utah State University, USA
Editor in Chief of the *International Journal of Multicultural Education*
Co-Author of *Our International Education: Living, Teaching, and Parenting Abroad*

"Engaging in autoethnography as writer, collaborator, and reader constitutes a transformative act of love, when love is understood – notably after bell hooks – as the willing act of nurturing compassionate, holistic, liberating and mutually respectful growth in self and others. Written by three well-respected, trailblazing experts of autoethnography, this important book is a gift to those willing to immerse themselves in the practical and life-changing power of the approach. At individual, group, organizational, institutional, and cultural levels, this has never been more necessary!"

Alec Grant, PhD
Unaffiliated Independent Scholar, UK
Recipient of the 2020 International Conference of Autoethnography
Lifetime Contribution Award

"*Transformative Autoethnography for Practitioners: Change Processes and Practices for Individuals and Groups* is a must-read for autoethnographic researchers. The captivating combination of a wealth of diverse insider experiences, passion and deep grasp of the challenges, opportunities and the subject literature ensures a perfect fit for the audience. The clear, inviting and confident writing style will inspire practitioners and novice researchers to work through the examples and templates as individuals or in collaboration with others. To embrace the enriching experience of transformative autoethnography (consequential or purposefully pursued) fully informed of the need to always strive for scientific rigor. I am looking forward to a new generation of transformative autoethnographic researchers and practitioners."

Ina Fourie, DLitt et Phil
Full professor, Head: Department of Information Science and Chair:
School of Information Technology University of Pretoria, South Africa

TRANSFORMATIVE AUTOETHNOGRAPHY FOR PRACTITIONERS

QUALITATIVE RESEARCH METHODOLOGIES: TRADITIONS, DESIGNS, AND PEDAGOGIES

EDITED BY KATHLEEN DEMARRAIS, MELISSA FREEMAN, JORI HALL, AND KATHRYN ROULSTON

The *Qualitative Research Methodologies: Traditions, Designs, and Pedagogies* series is designed to encourage qualitative researchers to look both backward and forward in the field of qualitative inquiry. We invite authors to submit proposals for both single-authored books and edited volumes focused on particular qualitative designs situated within their historical, theoretical, and disciplinary/cross-disciplinary contexts. Pieces might include a tradition's or design's historical roots and key scholars, ways the approach has changed over time, as well as ethical and methodological considerations in the use of that particular research approach. They may also provide an introduction to contemporary designs created at the intersection of multiple, theoretical, and often assumed incommensurable historical paths. In addition, we encourage authors to submit proposals for books focused on the pedagogy of qualitative research methodologies that interrogate how we prepare researchers new to qualitative research methodologies with the theoretical, methodological, and ethical understandings and skills for their work.

Those interested in being considered for inclusion in the series should send a prospectus (https://zfrmz.com/rmlvGq7xgL2RTgPkByk9), CV, and cover letter to: Kathleen deMarrais (kathleen@uga.edu).

Books in the Series:
Focus Groups: Culturally Responsive Approaches for Qualitative Inquiry and Program Evaluation
edited by Jori N. Hall (2020)
Exploring the Archives: A Beginner's Guide for Qualitative Researchers
by Kathryn Roulston and Kathleen deMarrais (2021)
Freirean Echoes: Multigenerational Dialogues in Contemporary Times
by Charlotte Achieng-Evensen, Kevin Stockbridge, Suzanne SooHoo (2021)
Transformative Autoethnography for Practitioners:
Change Processes and Practices for Individuals and Groups
by Kathy-Ann C. Hernandez, Heewon Chang, and Wendy A. Bilgen (2022)

TRANSFORMATIVE AUTOETHNOGRAPHY FOR PRACTITIONERS

∾ Change Processes and Practices for Individuals and Groups

BY KATHY-ANN C. HERNANDEZ,

HEEWON CHANG, AND WENDY A. BILGEN

Myers
Education
Press

Gorham, Maine

Copyright © 2022 | Myers Education Press, LLC
Published by Myers Education Press, LLC
P.O. Box 424
Gorham, ME 04038

Myers Education Press is an academic publisher specializing in books, e-books and digital content in the field of education. All of our books are subjected to a rigorous peer review process and produced in compliance with the standards of the Council on Library and Information Resources.

Library of Congress Cataloging-in-Publication Data available from Library of Congress.

13-digit ISBN 978-1-9755-0487-8 (paperback)
13-digit ISBN 978-1-9755-0488-5 (library networkable e-edition)
13-digit ISBN 978-1-9755-0489-2 (consumer e-edition)

Printed in the United States of America.

All first editions printed on acid-free paper that meets the American National Standards Institute Z39-48 standard.

Books published by Myers Education Press may be purchased at special quantity discount rates for groups, workshops, training organizations and classroom usage. Please call our customer service department at 1-800-232-0223 for details.

Cover design by Shelby Gates Newsted.

Visit us on the web at **www.myersedpress.com** to browse our complete list of titles.

Contents

List of Tables and Figures

Acknowledgments

WE BEGAN WRITING THIS BOOK during the global pandemic that began in 2019. This season of writing presented many challenges for us all as we navigated the other demands on our time as well as committing to this work. We are grateful to our family members who gave us space to write—they did not begrudge our closed office doors as we turned to our computers to write one more sentence, or one more paragraph. We are indebted to their love, care, patience, and trust in us.

I, Kathy-Ann, am grateful to my husband, Mark, for his loving support of my efforts that is evident in very practical ways. I owe him a debt of gratitude for doing the grocery shopping and driving the kids to their activities so that I could have some quiet time to write. I am also grateful to my daughters, Alyssa and Amya, who encourage me every day to continue to do the thing that I feel called to do—carve out a life path built on a legacy of words. Thank you for your love and support.

I, Heewon, want to express my enduring appreciation to my husband, Klaus Volpert, who has a profound understanding of the birthing pain that accompanies the labor of writing a book. Whenever my writing task was completed to my satisfaction, he always remembered to celebrate my success, whether it was over a cup of freshly brewed coffee or a sumptuous sushi dinner. I also acknowledge my grown-up children, Hannah and Peter, who have accomplished a lot in their lives but are still generous in giving compliments to their mom for doing "cool" things like writing a book. Their love and care, smiles and encouragement, and pride in me have kept me walking steadily in this writing journey.

In addition, I, Wendy, say thank you to my husband Haluk, whose belief in my abilities energizes me continually. Thank you also goes to my sons, Caleb and Benjamin, whose questioning minds and beautiful hearts keep me smiling when I feel weary. I am so very grateful to coauthors Heewon and Kathy-Ann for inviting me to write with them. Several years ago, when we first presented together at an academic conference, I remember feeling honored and apprehensive, wondering if I had something meaningful to add as the novice autoethnographer on the panel. Their belief that I do have something to add, then and now, has both delighted and encouraged me throughout this book project.

We also acknowledge and are grateful for two publisher colleagues: Mitch Allen and Chris Myers. Many good ideas of authors never appear to readers unless publishers believe in those ideas and are willing to take a risk in support of them. We are grateful to Dr. Mitch Allen for his support of autoethnography even beyond his publishing career. It was Mitch who introduced us to our current publisher, Chris Myers. We express our sincere appreciation to him for inviting us to dream of another autoethnography book. Thanks to his full trust in us, we are thrilled to bring this book to our readers.

In addition, we are especially grateful for the diligent editorial work of Dr. Linda Stine, a professor emeritus of writing at Lincoln University, USA, and former copy editor of the *International Journal of Multicultural Education*. She lent her keen editor's eyes in reviewing the final draft of this manuscript within a small window of time. Her generosity never fails and reminds us that good scholarship is built upon a community of caring friends and mentors. We also express sincere appreciation to our research assistant, Mrs. Lynnita Weber, who worked diligently behind the scenes conducting literature searches, compiling references, proofreading and editing our work, and offering constructive feedback. Her competent and timely work was critical in allowing us to meet publication deadlines.

Finally, we acknowledge rich contributions of fellow autoethnographers. The growing strength of autoethnography owes much to those who continue to push the boundaries of inquiry. We are grateful for the opportunity to build on their scholarship as they continue to inspire us with their stories, insights, and lessons. We humbly offer our work to the community of autoethnographer colleagues in the world.

Preface

SCHOLARSHIP IS NOT TRULY AN end in itself. We may embark on scholarship for a variety of reasons. Sometimes we are intent on provoking thought or formulating new theories to help us better understand more about the whys and hows of human experience. We may even advance political agendas and bring certain voices and issues to center stage through our scholarship. Ultimately, though, these purposes are not our final destination. The goal is to find strategies and solutions for dealing with the challenges we face within and beyond the academy. We research to understand social phenomena so that we can collectively live better lives.

As scholars and coauthors of this book, we believe in the value of scholarship for identifying problems so we can address some of the pressing issues of our time. In fact, we have spent much of our career doing just that, focusing on our respective areas of research in educational psychology, multicultural leadership education, and leadership studies. However, as we continue to mature in our scholarship and work with professional practitioners in various fields, we find ourselves positioned more squarely at the other end of the scholarship continuum—solution generation. This positioning requires us to ask and answer the "So what?" question. So what does this scholarship mean for practice? Writing this book has provided an opportunity for us to reflect on the journey towards our current positioning in scholarship and practice.

When each of us began our foray into the world of academia, we were drawn for various reasons at the intersection of who we were and the spaces in which we had lived. Together our experiences reveal some common themes. I (Kathy-Ann) was born in the twin island Republic of Trinidad and Tobago and migrated to the United States to pursue higher education. As an educator, I wanted to understand how to make teaching and learning more effective, especially for those who existed in marginal spaces in classrooms. Moreover, faced with what I was discovering about the inequities in academic spaces for people of color, I began to focus my research agenda and position myself as a scholar activist intent on provoking thought and facilitating action to create a more equitable academic landscape.

I (Heewon) grew up in Korea with a dream of becoming a teacher who could rebuild her postwar nation with a global understanding of democratic education benefiting all kinds of people. I moved to study educational anthropology and settled in the United States with the belief that democratic education would extend its benefit to all children globally. I extended my family connection to include not only Koreans and U.S.-Americans but also Germans. I am still maturing into my Korean-U.S.-German triple identity with the acknowledgment that my desire to make the world a better place needs to be grounded in continuous self-examination, global consideration, and ongoing confrontation of injustices around us. My work with organizational leaders in the Ph.D. program at my current university is a way to marry academics with praxis.

I (Wendy), a native of the United States, have been living in Turkey with my Turkish husband for the past two decades, raising our two sons and working as a therapist, educator, and mental health consultant. I began my career as a social worker compelled by a desire for *justice work*, although it has taken years for me to be able to articulate what that means. From my early experiences in the United States as a community and hospice social worker, later in Turkey as a crisis and trauma counselor and educator, to my more recent focus on leadership studies, one thing has remained clear: certain voices, namely, those of the marginalized in any cultural context, must find the space to speak more freely in order for personal healing and social innovation to be ignited in individuals and communities.

Our journeys have produced scholarship and practice in which we sought to effect these changes. More often than not, the pathway to getting there was not as direct as we had hoped. The targeted outcomes of our work were often couched in the language of "Implications of the Study." That began to change with our entry into the world of autoethnographic research. Unlike the work that dominated the early part of our careers, autoethnography invited us to situate ourselves quite visibly in our scholarship. What a welcome vantage point for research! Engagement in autoethnography pushed us to an intimate and richer level of interrogation of social phenomena that was soul-refreshing. However, what took us by surprise was that, while we found ourselves bringing a microscopic lens to our research that was inextricably connected to who we are, we also found that the process of engaging in this kind of research was life-changing. Our individual and sometimes collective experiences doing autoethnographic work proved to us that change or transformation did not have to wait for the end of the study; it was inherent in the autoethnographic method itself. Implications for practice did not have to be a serendipitous byproduct of the work, but a focal point! Moreover, the efficacy with which each of us had experienced this transformation provoked us to wonder if we could not envision a more direct route from scholarship to practice. What if the process were made transparent so that those inside and outside the academy could make use of autoethnography to experience the transformative benefits to themselves, those around them, and the spaces in which they were situated? What if? In this book we present a pathway for doing just that.

Transformative Autoethnography for Practitioners

Much has been written about autoethnography as a useful addition to the field of qualitative research methods. This approach to social inquiry continues to evolve as a valuable complement to existing research approaches. Autoethnography and its many applications across various disciplines provide ample evidence that the experiences of researchers as well as participants can contribute significantly to our understanding of social phenomena.

Whereas individual autoethnography centers the work of a single individual as both researcher and participant in an interrogation of self in relation to others, its variant, collaborative autoethnography, attempts to do the same in the company of others. Use of autoethnography has proliferated since the term first formally appeared in the 1970s. Since then, it has been extended across various disciplines including the humanities, human services, social sciences, leadership studies, engineering, education, counseling, and even medical education to name a few. Over the years, the primary function of autoethnography to advance our understanding around sociocultural phenomena has been increasingly paired with a parallel function of its many contributions to practice. Whereas its role in scholarship is well documented, less has been written about its practical usage as the focal point of inquiry. Yet, in our own work and in reading the scholarship of others, it is evident that one of the inherent strengths of autoethnography is the utility of the method to facilitate transformation of self, others, and organizations.

In this book, we turn the spotlight on autoethnography as a tool for practitioners who hope to solve real-life problems by facilitating transformational change at the individual, group, and/or organizational levels. To this end, we draw on existing scholarship as well as our collective work and expertise to offer a transformative autoethnographic model to practitioners who are intent on effecting such changes in their respective contexts.

How the Book Is Organized

The book contains seven chapters. Chapters One through Three provide the theoretical grounding for a transformative autoethnography model. In Chapter One, we begin with a broad overview of autoethnographic research and the unique characteristics of this method that makes it especially suited for effecting transformational learning. We also clarify what transformational learning is and what it is not. In Chapters Two and Three, we provide a quick review of the literature relevant to individual autoethnography and collaborative autoethnography respectively. Each chapter discussion is centered around explicating the transformative elements of the method as well as how it is able to effect change at the individual, group, and organizational level.

Chapters Four through Six focus on the praxis of transformative autoethnography. In Chapter Four, we present the transformative autoethnography model (TAM) in detail, as well as offer templates for its application in a variety of settings. With the use of visual models and templates, we show how the parallel functions of discovery and application work together in the TAM to strengthen and advance knowledge generation for and through transformation. In Chapters Five and Six, we discuss the application of the TAM in a variety of settings. Each of these chapters begins with some methodological considerations for use of the TAM. We then apply the model to three scenarios employing individual autoethnographic and collaborative autoethnographic methods in turn. In each case, we lean heavily on very practical examples. The book ends with a final chapter in which we discuss the continuing evolution of autoethnographic explorations, as well as future applications for the TAM model in a fast changing digital landscape.

How the Book Can Be Used

In writing this book, we have been mindful of you, the end user, and of how we could make the book accessible and easy to use. As a result, we have chosen a more relaxed tone in our writing. Each of the first four chapters and the final chapter of the book begins with a brief narrative of our individual experiences with autoethnography. We rely on the experiences of experts and other autoethnographers over the years to showcase the breadth and scope of autoethnographic practice. However, we also make use of our work to provide a unique insider perspective that informs the writing of this book.

We have intentionally structured it so you can easily find what you need. If you are looking for a practical guide on how to use autoethnography for individual and group transformation, you can focus your reading on Chapters Four through Six to understand the TAM model and to find practical guides, exercises, examples, and resources. If you are interested in the scholarly foundation for the transformative benefits of autoethnography, we make that case in Chapters One through Three of the book.

We are confident that the book contents, fully or partially used, will meet the needs of practitioners and scholars alike. We hope, though, that you commit to reading all chapters so you can gain a comprehensive understanding of transformative autoethnography and the path forward to engaging in this kind of life-changing work.

ONE

∾ Transformative Autoethnography

Heewon's Story

I HAD JUST WRAPPED UP A 15-minute conference presentation on my autoethnography work and was getting ready for the question and answer session that would follow. Before I could compose myself, a hand shot up from the audience. A smartly dressed gentleman asked:

"Should transformation be the goal of autoethnography?"

The question took me by surprise. I wanted to think about it some more and frame my response. However, since I had only five minutes to respond to questions posed by the gathering of about 25 attendees, I blurted out a quick response that the autoethnographic process changes people regardless of their goal or intent.

I realized that neither of us was satisfied with the brevity or the substance of my response, because after the session the gentleman found his way to me. I was more than eager to continue the conversation and glad for this opportunity to redeem myself. We chatted for a long time, not bothered by the fact that we were running late for the next session. From our conversation, I could tell that his question had not been challenging the legitimacy of autoethnography itself; in fact, he had himself recently published his own autoethnographic work. Rather, he was worried that the transformative intent of autoethnography could bias the autoethnographic research process itself. The question he wanted to ask was really a twofold one. First, should transformation be the goal of autoethnography? Second, could autoethnography lose its rigor and credibility as a social science research method for interrogating social phenomena to the practical goal of transformational learning? Since that encounter almost two decades ago, I have continued to ponder those two questions.

****

Much has been written about the transformative impact of the autoethnographic process before and after Heewon's encounter with that gentleman. A select list of publications, introduced and discussed in Chapters Two and

Three, attests to the popularity of autoethnographic use in academic inquiry. A quick read through some of these works reveals that, though not often intended, participants acknowledge the way or ways in which they were changed through the autoethnographic process. These sources of anecdotal evidence confirm that transformation, whether intended or not, is somehow part of the autoethnographic research experience. Thus, transformation emerges as a consequence of autoethnographic practice.

The real challenge then is to answer the hidden question posed by the gentleman at the conference. From a social science perspective, what might be the costs to an approach to social inquiry that moves away from social science knowledge generation to change-oriented praxis? Even those who might accept that researchers change as a result of learning from their research might be hesitant to plan for changes to researcher participants at the onset of social inquiry. Does purposeful transformation not belong to a different domain of activities, epistemologically and methodologically apart from pure research? Yet another question arises: Should autoethnographers' attention to transformative impacts and transformative purposes remain separate from their research process?

This book on the transformative autoethnography model (TAM) offers the possibility that consequential and purposeful transformation can coexist as important functions of autoethnographic practice. In fact, we argue that both functions augment each other within an integrated autoethnographic process to facilitate more relevant and meaningful impacts on autoethnographers and the ecological spaces in which they exist. Thus, we make the argument for the useful pairing of these autoethnographic functions and further explain the potential of autoethnographic work to accomplish both. This first chapter begins with a brief introduction to autoethnography as a research and praxis method and a description of the characteristics of autoethnographic research. This is followed by a conceptual discussion of *self-reflexivity* as the core activity in the autoethnographic process. Finally, we highlight the potential of authoethnographic research to facilitate both *consequential* and *purposeful* transformation at the personal and communal level.

What Is Autoethnography?

Autoethnography is not a new genre of research or writing. It first appeared in anthropology literature (Hayno, 1979), originating from the anthropological tradition of ethnography. Since then it has evolved as one of many qualitative research methods adopted in a wide range of social, natural, and health science fields. Today it is both fast-growing and perhaps the most contested qualitative research approach.

Autoethnography can be described as a researcher-focused qualitative research method that utilizes the researcher's autobiographical experiences as the primary data in an attempt to gain a sociocultural understanding of their lived experiences in relation to others and their contexts (Adams et al., 2014; Chang, 2008, 2016; Ellis et al., 2011; Hughes & Pennington, 2016; Poulos, 2021; Reed-Danahay, 1997/2021). Autoethnographic work is traditionally conducted by one individual who is both researcher and participant in investigating social phenomena. However, autoethnography can also be done in groups.

In this book, we use *autoethnography* as a categorical term encompassing all varieties of autoethnography, while the term *individual autoethnography* (IAE) is used when we need to differentiate individual works from the group endeavors, as indicated by *collaborative autoethnography* (CAE). Individual autoethnography and collaborative autoethnography share common methodological tenets of autoethnography but also present distinctive strengths and challenges respectively. The proliferation of published autoethnographies makes it impossible to provide a fair representation of each variety in this book; thus, only selected examples are presented. While autoethnography, done alone or in the company of others, may be simply thought of as *self ethnography*, emphasizing "self" (Ellis, 2004, p. 43), it still conforms to the normative expectations of social science research practice intent on a deeper understanding of sociocultural phenomena.

Since autoethnography first appeared as an approach that elevates the power of the researcher's personal story in inquiry, it has continued to evolve with diverse definitions and applications. Its usage has been extended across various disciplines including the humanities, human services, social sciences, leadership studies, engineering, education, counseling, and even medical education, to name a few, with much variability in approaches and usage (Chang, 2021; 2022). Such widespread usage attests to the malleability of the research method and its unique contributions to scholarship and practice.

Different Approaches to Autoethnography

Different terms have been used to label autoethnographic works. That is because the autoethnographic process and product often take on inquirers' dominant or mixed preferences and the nomenclature used to describe the work is often reflective of their preferences. *Evocative* and *analytic autoethnography* exemplify two conceptually contrasting approaches, although in practice they can intermingle or coexist in one autoethnography work.

Evocative autoethnographies invite readers to enter into the experiences of the researchers—to evoke an emotional response from them based on the commonality of human experience. Bochner and Ellis (2016), leading scholars of this approach, suggested that autoethnography elicits this kind of response in others as it "shows struggle, passion, embodied life, and the collaborative creation of sense-making in situations in which people have to cope with dire circumstances and loss of meaning" (p. 433). In evocative autoethnography, the writer attempts to capture the essence of the researcher's lived experiences with the expressed intent of evoking a response/reaction in the reader. Although analysis takes place as the researcher makes meaning and engages in storying of the experience, no explicit attempt is typically made to formally analyze the study findings beyond what is expressed in storytelling. The presentation of individual and collaborative autoethnographic work that is evocative in nature can also take myriad forms, including poetry, prose, dance, spoken word, music, and performing art. In that regard, such pieces often reject traditional forms of social writing and inquiry opting to "be unruly, dangerous, vulnerable, rebellious, and creative" and nonconforming to the dictates of reason, logic and analysis (p. 433). This means that more flexibility in expression is usually afforded in evocative autoethnography.

Alternatively, some researchers take a distinct analytical approach, drawing on best practices from the field of social science research to conceptualize, conduct, and report the study findings (Ngunjiri et al., 2010). Anderson (2006), in a critique of the self-focused aspect of autoethnography, called for an analytical approach that conformed to the dictates of social inquiry. He advocated for autoethnography to be more consistent with the goals of ethnography—to offer commentary on social phenomena. He argued that "autoethnography loses its sociological promise when it devolves into self-absorption" (p. 385). Similarly, Atkinson (2006) advocated for the goals of "analysis and theorizing" to remain central to the ethnographic approach to autoethnographic work (p. 400). The analytic approach was also advanced in the book *Collaborative Autoethnography* (Chang et al., 2013) and various publications (see Hernandez et. al., 2014; Ngunjiri et. al., 2010).

Many other categorical labels have been employed to describe diverse autoethnographic approaches. In addition to the evocative and narrative approach (Bochner & Ellis, 2016) and the analytic one (Anderson, 2006; Chang, 2008; Fourie, 2021), other approaches have been offered such as the interpretive (Denzin, 2014; Ellis, 1998; Ramírez-Pereira et al., 2018), the critical (Boylorn & Orbe, 2020), and the performative (Denzin, 2018; Holman Jones, 2018; Ramírez-Pereira et al., 2018; Spry, 2017). Chang (2008) also offered a list of almost 40 labels that researchers used to describe their autoethnography or autoethnography like work (pp. 47–48) and typologized autoethnographic writing into four approaches: descriptive-realistic, confessional-emotive, analytic-interpretive, and imaginative-creative. In comparison, Adams and Manning (2015) distinguished between social-scientific, interpretive-humanistic, critical, and creative-artistic (dramatic or evocative) autoethnographies.

Even a cursory review of the literature will show that authors of many publications have debated about categorizations of autoethnographies and expressed their preference over the analytical or the evocative approach. We steer clear of such debates and unhelpful dichotomies. Rather, we acknowledge that while "these orientations can influence how a researcher understands, designs, and evaluates an autoethnographic project" (Adams & Manning, 2015, p. 352), various orientations often overlap within the same work. Whichever labels autoethnographers elect to use to describe their works, effective transformative autoethnographies are likely to present revelatory analysis and relevant interpretation, combined with emotionally evocative, precise, and purposeful storytelling, to assist readers with the sociocultural understanding of the autoethnographers' lived experiences within their context.

Characteristics of Autoethnography

As part of the methodological family of qualitative inquiry methods, autoethnography shares some common characteristics with other qualitative research methods. Yet variations within autoethnographic works, as noted in the previous section, can easily overwhelm autoethnographers' confidence in using this method. Here we offer some defining features of this method across variations: namely, autoethnographies (1) pursue an in-depth understanding of sociocultural phenomena as an inquiry method; (2) capture personal experiences through the power of storying; (3) utilize autoethnographers' personal experiences as primary data; (4) offer autoethnographers the options of conducting the interrogation individually or collaboratively; (5) engage the autoethnographic process for both research and praxis purposes; and (6) result in diverse forms of autoethnographic products, such as written texts, embodied performances, virtual representations, or other creative products. Each feature is discussed in more detail in this section. We also use more inclusive terms such as *inquirers* and *autoethnographers*, instead of *researchers*, to include both researchers and practitioners of autoethnography.

Inquiry Method for In-Depth Understanding

Autoethnography is an inquiry method through which inquirers seek an understanding of a selected sociocultural phenomenon through the intentional and systematic process of gathering, analyzing, and interpreting data. This method can be used in both formal research or informal inquiry contexts. Like other research methods in the social sciences, autoethnographic research involves formal and informal data collection, analysis, interpretation, and reporting of findings. However, these steps are conducted consistent with nuances unique to this genre and its many variations.

Autoethnography encourages the use of the whole self throughout the research process, as it is a methodology of thinking, feeling, sensing, questioning, challenging, and understanding self, others, and society. Autoethnographers are unapologetic about the ways in which their research interests reflect personal inquiries into cultural identity, power struggles, social injustice, race, and gender relations. In particular, those engaged in critical autoethnography courageously confront very powerful social and political structures in their own lives. As a form of ethnography that often results in products that seem more like art than science, autoethnography does not fit neatly into past frameworks of systematic rigor for qualitative inquiry. This seeming "unfitness" often puts autoethnographers in conflict with conventional social scientists and even with other qualitative researchers (Coffey, 1999; Poulos, 2020; Stahlke Wall, 2016). However, this methodological tension also provides autoethnographers with freedom to innovate and experiment in scientific liminality.

Despite varying approaches, as noted previously, all processes follow the systematic inquiry path to produce trustworthy and reliable conclusions. The term *systematic*, as used here, does not imply that all autoethnography must follow the formalized data analysis and interpretation approach of conventional social science research. Rather, it highlights that autoethnographic processes or production are neither haphazard nor compulsive.

Use of Personal Experience as Primary Data

Unlike other qualitative research methods, autoethnography uniquely uses the inquirer's personal experiences as primary data, which serve as an entryway to the in-depth understanding of selected sociocultural phenomena. Individual personal data is rich because we are all social beings embedded in webs of relationships with others within sociocultural contexts. Inquirers have unfettered access to this personal repository of experiences in the quarry of primary data (Adams et al., 2021; Hughes & Pennington, 2016; Poulos, 2021). Who has better access to this data mining, outsiders or insiders? Autoethnography privileges the insider positionality of inquirers to investigate personal experiences at a depth that outside researchers cannot easily reach.

Contrary to common thinking, interrogation of self is not simplistic. Rather, as complex beings, we all exist in intricate webs of relationships situated in varied social contexts. Hence, the exploration of self involves the study of the intersecting and combinational implications of inquirers' experiential, relational, and contextual data. Therefore, as these data are analyzed and interpreted holistically, the sociocultural meaning of these personal experiences can be uncovered. Connecting the personal with the social is the fundamental tenet of autoethnography (Adams et al., 2014; Chang, 2013; Ellis et al., 2011; Poulos, 2021; Reed-Danahay, 1997/2021). This point is elaborated on further in the next section focusing on self-reflexivity.

Storying of Personal Experiences

The storying process is a central mechanism of autoethnographic work. Many who are drawn to autoethnography see the power of the story as one of the most potent distinctives. For example, Holman Jones (2008) elaborated on the storied nature of autoethnography as follows:

> Autoethnography is setting a scene, telling a story, weaving intricate connections among life and art, experience and theory, evocation and explanation . . . and then letting it go, hoping for readers who will bring the same careful attention to your words in the context of their own lives. (p. 208)

Their description of storying, however, affirms that autoethnography is more than mere storytelling. Whether evocative or analytical, it is purposeful. Autoethnographic stories can be used to give voice to "previously silenced and marginalized experiences . . . answer unexamined questions about the multiplicity of social identities, instigate discussion about and across differences, and explain the contradictory intersections of personal and cultural standpoints" (Boylorn & Orbe, 2014, p. 15). The role of story is embedded in both the autoethnographic process and product.

While personal narrative, particularly the author's story, is a focus in all autoethnographic work, *narrative* and *story* have distinctive characteristics as applied to autoethnographic work. Narrative can be considered the specific words that are used to describe an experience, while story is the intentional way those words are arranged, in a specific scheme that brings out meaning (Frank, 2009). It is stories that "work on people, because people become caught up in stories to a degree that is exceptional" (Frank, 2010, p. 665). Even though there is transformative potency in well-presented personal stories through a variety of autoethnographic and performative products, autoethnography involves more than sensationalized storytelling without analysis (Ellis, 2004). Autoethnographers are challenged to be both *story analysts*, concerned with facts, and *storytellers*, concerned with meaning (Bochner, 2010).

Individual or Collaborative Interrogation

Autoethnography can be conducted by individual autoethnographers in solo efforts or by groups of autoethnographers in collaborative projects. The authorship of autoethnography typically identifies a work as an individual autoethnography (IAE) or a collaborative autoethnography (CAE). Namely, IAEs tend to be published by single authors (e.g., Bhattacharya, 2018; Hunter, 2020; O'Connell, 2021), whereas CAEs are coauthored by two or more authors (e.g., Chang et al., 2014; Hernandez, et al., 2015; Zou et al., 2020). These are but a few examples.

In the case of some collaborative autoethnographies, it is possible that not all authors are autoethnographers who contributed their personal experiences to the collaborative work. For example, not all autoethnographers contributed their personal stories to a CAE project centering leaders of color in higher education (Chang et al., 2014; Longman et al., 2015). Longman and Chang led the collaborative autoethnographic process as research coaches but did not contribute their own autobiographic data to their engaged research project. In some duo-authored work, partial collaboration is also present. For example, Rawicki contributed his holocaust survival stories whereas Ellis assisted the collaborative process as a researcher (Ellis & Rawicki, 2013); similarly, Lowe, the researcher, assisted Yarborough to bring out his family business dilemma story as his coresearcher (Yarborough & Lowe, 2007). As the examples of IAEs and CAEs in Chapters Two and Three demonstrate, this characteristic of versatility offers autoethnographers various options to explore sociocultural phenomena from the vantage point of personal experiences.

Process for Research and Praxis

Autoethnography has expanded its usefulness not only in research but also in professional practice since it began as a research method in the 1970s. Individual autoethnography and its variant, collaborative autoethnography, have been recognized for their unique positioning in the social science landscape and for their ability to straddle the lines of scholarship and praxis applications. For example, while attending to knowledge-generation relevant to social phenomena, autoethnographic research has also facilitated the following: creating supportive learning communities that foster personal and professional learning and development (Blalock & Akehi, 2018; Longman et al., 2015); providing insider perspectives to intimate issues (Norwood, 2018; Tillmann, 2009); positioning multivocality as a necessary element in the practice of social inquiry and theory building (Ngunjiri et al., 2017); challenging positivist paradigms of what is truth and what is worth studying (Adams et al., 2021; Holman Jones et al., 2015); and linking research methods across different disciplines (Hernandez, 2021). The capacity of autoethnography to accomplish all this sets it apart as a research method.

A large body of praxis-oriented autoethnographies is dedicated to demonstrating the potential of autoethnography for professional development.

Selected application fields include teacher development (Canagarajah, 2012; Pinner, 2018), university human resource development (Chang et al., 2014, O'Neil, 2018), athletic and sports leader development (Preston & Fraser-Thomas, 2018), community leader development (Kniffin et al., 2021), healthcare professional development (Acosta et al., 2015; Taylor et al., 2008), and human service professional development (Jensen-Hart & Williams, 2010; McIlveen, 2008). All of these applications emphasize the importance of critical self-reflexivity in the development of reflective professionals.

Diverse Autoethnographic End Products

The autoethnographic inquiry process is expected to lead to autoethnographic production. Ellis et al. (2011) argued that "autoethnography is both process and product" (p. 273). Autoethnographic products span a broad continuum of more evocative to more analytical approaches. Some autoethnography end products look more like art than science: narrative (Shepherd et al., 2020), poetry (Faulkner, 2017), theatrical scripts (Alexander et al., 2015), embodied performance (Carless & Douglas, 2021; Spry, 2001), visual presentations (Scarles, 2010), and multimedia presentation (Cormier, 2020). Other autoethnographic products resemble traditional deliverables from the social sciences—scholarly reports, articles, and presentations.

Typically the written texts, often presented in prose, dominate the autoethnography literature; however, some autoethnographies have engaged the combination of different formats in their autoethnographic products. All of the examples represent polished final products that were intended for public dissemination. However, some autoethnographies are done for private use. These can take the form of personal essays, reflective journals, testimonies, or action plans. They may be kept for personal consumption or small-group audiences only.

Self-Reflexivity at the Core of Autoethnography

Autoethnographers engage self-reflexivity as the central mode of investigation. Self-reflexivity refers to "the process of looking at the self" (Moriera, 2011, p. 148) or "the careful consideration of the ways in which researchers' past experiences, points of view, and roles impact these same researchers' interactions with, and interpretations of, the research scene" (Poulos, 2021, p. 5). Both definitions acknowledge looking at the self at the center of self-reflexive activities; however, neither stops at a perpetual cycle of navel-gazing nor microscopic zooming in on self in isolation. Instead, self-reflexivity, evident in Poulos's definition, is considered as a dialogical process in which one holistically and critically examines self within the relational context with others. This definition points to four characteristics of self-reflexivity: (1) engaging deeper examination of the self; (2) examining the self in relation to others within their contexts; (3) making honest and transparent efforts to discover new insights about the self in deeper levels; and (4) motivating self-improvement and actionable changes. Each characteristic of self-reflexivity is further explained here.

Deeper Examination of Self

Self-reflexivity moves beyond reflection, recollection, and introspection to reach a deeper level of self-learning through self-observation, self-analysis, self-critique, and self-appraisal. Ploder and Stadlbauer (2016) affirmed this position that self-reflexivity is not "mere descriptions of experiences and feelings, an inner monologue, a stream-of-consciousness depiction of mental, physical, or emotional experiences [that] can be completely non-reflexive" (p. 754). Instead, it allows us to critically examine our lives, evaluate our assumptions and *weltanschauung* (worldview); and conduct "self-appraisal" about our own identities and positionalities about life around us (Koopman et al., 2020, p. 1).

Autoethnographers do not merely gaze on their past experiences. As they examine these experiences, they ask themselves repeatedly if they have "penetrated as many layers" of their own "defenses, fears, and insecurities" as the project requires. This kind of deep self-interrogation ultimately challenges their assumptions, beliefs, perspectives, and actions (Ellis, 2016, p. 10). Namely, self-reflexivity engages deeper examination of the self.

Examination of Self in Relation to Others

Second, self-reflexivity moves the autoethnographic interrogation beyond self-centric isolation that could potentially lead to narcissistic or self-indulgent navel gazing. Although self-reflexivity begins with understanding ourselves, it contextualizes our personal experiences in relation to others and their sociocultural surroundings. Self-reflexivity in autoethnographic work then challenges inquirers to examine themselves in relation to others.

The self-other relationship can be conceptualized in different ways. For example, Chang (2008) referred to others as other beings outside the self. She typologized others into three categories: "others of similarity" who share similar values and are more intimately connected to the self; "others of difference" who have different or unfamiliar experiences and/or worldviews than the self; and "others of opposition" who stand in oppositional positions from the self (pp. 26–28). According to Chang, we are in direct or indirect interaction with various others, and the contexts in which we share with others influence our experiences. Whereas Chang focused on physical others outside the self, Hermans (2001) emphasized how others take internal and external positions within the self in his dialogical self theory (DST). Others become part of the self as the voices of others take specific positions in the memories and internal psychological spaces of the self. The self, according to DST, is conceived as a dynamic collective of internal and external voices influenced by dialogic interaction with others in specific cultural contexts (Hermans & Hermans-Konopka, 2010). Whether others reside outside or inside of the self, self-reflexivity pulls others into their relational examination of the self.

Reflexivity allows us to shift our gazes between inward and outward looks to discover the sociocultural meaning of our personal experiences in relation to others. Wiesner (2020) called this shifting gaze of autoethnography "a transpersonal approach" that would enable autoethnographers to gain a "holistic perspective on events that have already happened or are happening in our life" but to lift this inquiry method above the arena of "too personal and, therefore, too narrow" (p. 665). Therefore, through sound reflexivity, autoethnography overcomes the potential "evil of narcissistic navel-gazing" (Ploder & Stadlbauer, 2016, p. 755). In addition, the autoethnographic consideration of sociocultural contexts elevates personal experiences as social phenomena. This assumption is foundational in social science research. Otherwise, the collection of data from research participants is meaningless. The sociocultural context, where the self and others cohabit and interact, is a critical element to consider in autoethnographic holism.

Honest and Transparent Self-Discovery

Self-reflexivity requires honest and transparent efforts in the self-discovery process. Reflexivity is particularly critical to qualitative researchers because of the significant influence they have on their research process and product through using the self as a reference point. It is necessary then for researchers to continually "bend back" upon themselves when considering an idea or thought with regard to the research content and process. They must ask themselves critical questions about what their own subjectivity is doing to the inquiry process and products. For this, Berger (2015) articulated the importance of the researcher's honest acknowledgement:

> Researchers need to increasingly focus on self-knowledge and sensitivity; better understand the role of the self in the creation of knowledge; carefully self-monitor the impact of their biases, beliefs, and personal experiences on their research; and maintain the balance between the personal and the universal. (p. 220)

Therefore, transparency about their own positionality is expected to achieve credibility and trustworthiness of their research process. Koopman et al. (2020) affirmed this role of reflexivity in the self-acknowledgment of the ultrasubjective process:

> Reflexivity is . . . often described as the process of a continual internal dialogue and critical self-evaluation of researchers' positionality . . . . Reflexivity compels us to confront the choices we make regarding the research question, the people we involve in the research process, and the multiple identities that we bring and create in the research setting . . . . The ideal for reflexivity is that this self-appraisal be actively acknowledged and openly recognizable in the research process and product. (p. 1)

Since the autoethnographic process is riddled with many personal choices by the investigators, the open process of self-reflexivity calls for the honest and transparent questioning of their own subjectivity. It is the self-reflexivity that makes the autoethnographic process trustworthy and credible.

Catalyst for Self-improvement and Change

Self-reflexivity is a catalyst for self-improvement and actionable changes. The self-reflexive journey takes individuals on a path of self-examination and self-evaluation in relation to others and contexts to deeper self-learning and discovery. This intimate exploration into the self is likely to inspire changes toward further development and improvement. Feucht et al. (2017) argued that reflexivity as

> an internal dialogue . . . leads to action for transformative practices in the classroom . . . when informed and intentional internal dialogue leads to changes in educational practices, expectations, and beliefs. Reflexivity can promote deep professional learning and bring sustainable change in education. (p. 234)

Self-discovery as a result of self-reflexivity inspires autoethnographers to use knowledge gains and insights of the self as catalysts for renewal, reform, or redirection for their development. The transformative power of autoethnography is frequently noted in the autoethnography literature, as demonstrated amply in Chapters Two and Three.

Self-reflexivity, the core driving force behind the autoethnographic process, is characterized as an intentional activity that interlaces the inward self-reflection with the outward examination of self-other relationships within their contexts. It requires honest and transparent exploration for any meaningful relational and contextual self-discovery and inspires transformation at various levels and in diverse forms. The nature of autoethnography-inspired transformation is explained in greater depth in the following section.

The Transformative Power of Autoethnography

Autoethnographers, who use their own story to lay bare the topics of their research through self-reflexivity, grapple with the question "Toward what end?" or "What work does it do?" (Gale & Wyatt, 2019, p. 566). This question asks for connections between the autoethnographers' personal stories and the meanings of their lived experiences as sociocultural phenomena. It is the "so what?" question. What does this mean for scholarship and/or for practice? The answer to the question relative to autoethnographic work is simply this: We engage in autoethnography to discover something new about ourselves and others through our personal experiences with self and others in context. The process and end products of such self-explorations have the capacity to transform us and those around us.

Much has been written about the transformative impact of autoethnography (Glowacki-Dudka et al., 2005; Kiesinger, 2002). Many more examples are provided in the following chapters. But "What is transformation?" and "What does autoethnography have to do with transformation?" When the word *transformation* and its many other derivatives—*transformative*, or *transformational*, or *transforming*—are used in social sciences, they mean substantial and sustainable changes in many different ways. MacGregor Burns (2003) defined *transformation* as "metamorphosis in form or structure, a change in the very condition or nature of a thinking, a change into another substance, a radical change in outward form or inner character" in the context of transformative leadership (p. 24). Although this definition originated specific to a social science concept, it is applicable to transformative autoethnography. We have defined *transformation* in the context of this book as substantial and potentially sustainable change in knowledge, insights, and/or behaviors that can take place in individuals, communities, and organizations through the process of autoethnographic inquiry. It is any change, whether slow and incremental or sudden and full-bodied, that is felt, seen, embodied, and acted upon at various levels. Consistent with principles of transformative learning, such change/s can take place in an individual's life through the application of autoethnography.

Our use of the term *transformation* builds on the work of a variety of scholars. In particular it is consistent with tenets of transformative learning theory as it was applied to adult education through the work of Jack Mezirow (1997, 2000). Mezirow's thoughts about transformative processes were grounded in the work of other philosophers and educators. Mezirow drew from Kuhn's (1962) *paradigm theory*, Freire's (1970) *conscientization*, and Habermas's (1984) *domains of learning*. While Mezirow's work focused mainly on individual perspective change in adult learners, an embedded assumption in his theorizing is that individual perspective change would inevitably lead to wide-reaching change in society.

Expanding on the notion that transformative learning does not end with individual perspective change, Hoggan (2016) suggested that transformative learning be considered a metatheory "under which individual theories aggregate" (p. 70). Hoggan presented a typology that could help gauge the reach of transformation beyond individual perspective change and widen the scope of transformative learning "to processes that result in significant and irreversible changes in the way a person experiences, conceptualizes, and interacts with the world" (p. 71). Transformation can be both subjectively understood (where one identifies a fresh or enlightened understanding), and objectively seen and felt, sometimes even measured by others (Mezirow & Associates, 1990). And while transformative learning as a theory originated and "finds its home within adult education," the expansion of the theory and "intersection with other ways of thinking about transformation and development" (Schapiro et al., 2017, p. 9) is expressed in many disciplines, including through the practice of autoethnography.

Transformative learning understood this way invites a range of experiences and outcomes across disciplines. For example, transformation in counseling and psychotherapy might be characterized by cycles of *rupture and repair*. A rupture entails a disorienting event(s), often a result of trauma, challenge, or suffering, followed by a process of repair facilitated by a therapist who helps the client through healing, growth, and eventually a change in condition and behavior. Transformation might be recognized in the mind (thoughts and mental modes), emotions (what one feels), bodily (physicality), consciousness (spiritual, transcendent), and might be measured in various ways by a clinician (Ross, 2020). Kegan (2000) has referred to the various manifestations of transformation as human "forms that transform" (p. 35) suggesting that one can be explicit regarding what form undergoes fundamental change during human transformation.

Transformation could be explored from various perspectives: levels, domains, forms, and extent. Transformation could occur at different levels (e.g., personal, organizational, or societal) or in different domains (e.g., cognitive, affective, behavioral, operational, and structural). At the personal level, for example, changes could occur in the cognitive domain such as knowledge gains, insight, perspective shifts, frame of reference, or worldview; in the behavioral domain changes could arise in behavior, action, habit, or skill; or in the affective domain in feeling, emotion, attachment, or preference. When changes occur at an organizational level, they can happen in an invisible domain such as mission, culture, value, and priority; in an operational domain such as operational practice, policies, and regulations; and in a structural domain such as organizational systems and positional structures. Kegan (2018) introduced yet another language of transformation, namely, "forms that transform" (p. 35). For example, he noted that some forms—artistic, performative, emotional, and sensual—may focus on the "transport" (Tisdell, 2012, p. 22) of hearts, moods, thoughts, or the way of being in our social world (Kegan, 2000; Mezirow, 1991), whereas other forms may focus on transforming the social and cultural world itself, upending norms and challenging systems of oppression in what has been called *emancipatory* change (Diversi & Moreira; 2018; Horton & Freire, 1990). The diversity of transformation also exists in terms of the extent of changes. While some changes may come gradually when the old norms are modified, expanded, or reduced incrementally, other changes may come drastically when the new normal is introduced suddenly as a result of societal disruption or innovation.

Although the definitions vary, we will focus on the fundamental tenet of transformation as significant shifts in cognitive, affective, spiritual, psychological, and/or behavioral domains of individuals, communities, and/or organizations. We have argued that the self-reflexive process of autoethnography can generate this type of deep transformation. In this section, the transformative power of autoethnography is discussed in three areas: (1) transformation to autoethnographers (at the personal level of the self); (2) transformation to readers and audiences of autoethnographies (at the personal level of others); and (3) transformation to the present and future contexts involving the self and others (at the organizational and societal level). Each point is elaborated further in the following paragraphs.

Transformation to Autoethnographers

Transformation can take place within autoethnographers themselves. In the process of closely observing and analyzing their personal data, they may experience a series of passages or movements through one understanding about themselves to another. These moments may be experienced as gradual or sudden shifts in self-discovery. These "passages" are often associated with crisis, epiphany, or the slower processes of incremental change, like maturation and aging.

The autoethnography literature is replete with rich transformative accounts at the personal level. Due to the large volume of such works, only a few examples are presented here: e.g., death (Whalen & Simmons, 2021), divorce (Dunn, 2020), health crisis (Nowakowski & Sumerau, 2019), immigration (Gnanadass et al., 2021), coming-out with same-sex attraction (Adams, 2012), religious conversion (Poplin, 2011), and promotion to a new leadership role (Walford, 2004). Additional examples can be found in Chapters Two and Three. Some changes are culturally supported markers of outward and visible transitions whereas others may accompany internal transformation that is less visible, and perhaps purposefully hidden. Big and small, drastic and gradual, obvious and subtle, conscious and unconscious, unintended and purposeful, transformation to autoethnographers is accomplished through their self-reflexive process.

In many instances in published works, authors note that such discoveries were not often intended or planned (see Chapters Two and Three). However, with intentionality such changes could be explicitly or implicitly noted before or after transformative events. Changes may be identified with regards to the nature and/or the extent of the person's cognitive, affective, behavioral, physical, social, or even spiritual changes by the events.

Transformation to Readers and Audiences

Transformation also happens to others—readers or audiences of autoethnography—when autoethnographers cocreate an emotionally shared space through their stories. Tisdell's (2021) concept of transport may apply here. By reading or watching autoethnographic products, readers or audiences are often drawn to empathize with the autoethnographers' lived experiences, emotionally interact with the texts or performances, and consequently experience the transformation of their own perspectives, insights, knowledge, and behaviors. When an authoethnographer's individual experiences are shared and empathized within the common historical, social, and cultural space, autoethnography is able to touch the souls of consumers. This phenomenon of emanating transformation can be illustrated with the following example. When listening to the compelling testimony of someone else's experiences, one may feel the power of the individual narrative to shift meaning in the listener. Speaking specifically of the testimonial literature of Anzaldua, Keating and González-López (2011) said:

> We believe that radical transformation begins with the personal but must move outward, linking self-change with social change. We, too, believe in the possibility of converting even our most difficult, painful situations and events into powerful lessons that can be applied to our lives, shared with others, and used to enact multilevel transformation. (p. 2)

Autoethnography offers a tool to first interrogate our own experiences toward the transformation of existing knowledge systems and social structures (Diversi & Moreira, 2018). However, the transformative impact of autoethnography does not stop there. Instead, Bochner and Ellis (2016) argued that "autoethnography is not a spectator sport" and therefore compels audience participation (p. vii). Holman Jones (2005) echoed that autoethnography as a "personal text can move writers and readers, subjects and objects, tellers and listeners into [a] space of dialogue, debate, and change" (p. 764). The acknowledged goal of autoethnographic research, albeit not always explicitly stated in the product, "is not [only] to describe, reconstruct, or ultimately understand, but rather to change social reality" (Ploder & Stadlbauer, 2016, p. 754). If done well, no individual, group, or system comes out of an autoethnographic process untouched, and therein lies its transformative power. This kind of emanating transformation from the self to others is typically unexpected because autoethnographers do not engineer the direction or intensity of transformation to others from the beginning. With or without a transformative intent, however, they can create the conditions for transformation to take place. Even when they do not possess the capacity to control the where, why, and how of the transformation in others, transformation can occur consequently. This is mostly likely to be the case when autoethnographies touch consumers organically.

Transformation for the Present and Future

Autoethnography has the potential to have transformative impacts on the contexts that autoethnographers and others tangibly and conceptually cohabitate. For example, contextual transformation through autoethnography has been observed in the context of organizations as well as the broader society (Boyle & Parry, 2007; Herrmann, 2020; López & Tracy, 2020; Sambrook & Herrmann, 2018). For example, Oswald et al. (2020) illustrated how autoethnography was used to challenge organizational cultural and structural status quo that perpetuated unfair practices to doctoral students; similarly, Zawadzki and Jensen (2020) challenged the "bullying" behaviors prevalent in academia against junior scholars. Looking beyond the organizational changes through autoethnography, Tisdell (2012) paid attention to the utility of autoethnography as a means for social changes beyond personal changes:

> Some change our hearts forever as they transform our identity as a core theme. Others, in their many variations, bring us into a larger consciousness as we forge new patterns of connections that change the vibration of our cells and our souls, our brains and our beings. Still others happen when we summon the courage to stand up to power, on behalf of ourselves and others, to create a more just world. (p. 34)

Particularly, critical autoethnography aims at promoting transformation of particular social and political conditions (Boylorn & Orbe, 2020). Critical autoethnographers use their own subjective experiences to challenge the "taken for granted master narratives about how life is or is supposed to be" (Short et al., 2013, p. 4) in order to question and critique dominant cultural meanings.

Many autoethnographers specifically choose *critical* autoethnographic methodology in pursuit of a social change or justice agenda, with the aim of scrutinizing and critiquing social and organizational practices (Boylorn & Orbe, 2020). Even many who do not name their autoethnographic approach as *critical* identify transformation as a welcome result of the autoethnographic process (Diversi & Moreira, 2018; Poulos, 2019; Reed-Danahay, 2017; Short et al., 2013). As Holman Jones et al. (2015) argued, autoethnographers offer firsthand accounts of their personal stories as opportunities for "representing, breaking, and remaking" their own understanding of personal experiences as well as systemic practices (p. 39). By intentionally tackling sensitive topics and controversial positions which are often ignored, distorted, or silenced in traditional research, autoethnography offers transformative opportunities to organizational and social contexts (Berry et al., 2019; Turner et al., 2018).

In sum, autoethnographic transformation can be exhibited in many different ways. Although three types of transformation—to self, to others, and to contexts—are discussed separately, transformation at any level is likely to overlap to other levels. Transformation at personal levels inspires or motivates transformation to others and contexts. Diversi et. al. (2020) explained the nature of autoethnography as a "betweener" form of inquiry (p. 15): it sits like a bridge between connecting personal accounts with wider cultural, political, and social realities, while it also sits between artistic form and social science report. Therefore, the transformative power of autoethnography must be understood holistically, as we need to understand self-reflexivity as an interactive dance among self, others, and contexts.

Consequential Versus Purposeful Transformation

Transformation to individuals, others, or organizations is well acknowledged as a natural byproduct of autoethnography in published research. This kind of transformation can be described as consequential transformation and is acknowledged in Sykes's (2014) notion of "transformative autoethnography." Consequential transformation is often visibly recognizable but not purposefully engineered or intentionally designed, because a transformative intent is viewed as a threat to rigorous social inquiry methods.

The question the scholar posed to Heewon, referenced at the beginning of this chapter, reflects this underlying fear of bias-contamination in social science research. Despite such a fear, various forms of self-narrative methods, including autoethnography, have used personal experiences for self-discovery and inspired intentional self-transformation, particularly for professional development, in many practitioner-dominant social science fields. They include education (Canagarajah, 2012; Pinner, 2018), social work (Jensen-Hart & Williams, 2010), nursing care (Acosta et al., 2015), and leadership (Chang et al., 2014). Although not all of the publications are labeled as autoethnography and they represent a wide range of transformative intent, content, process, and outcome, all used self-discovery as a tool for emancipatory transformative learning that was designed to improve practice for professional development (Horton & Friere, 1990; Mezirow, 1991; Tisdell, 2012). It is this uncovering of the praxis intent in autoethnographic work that is the impetus for this book. Particularly, we advance a praxis-oriented transformative model of learning purposefully, which integrates the *transformative intent* into the learning process to improve practitioners' relational understanding of others within their professional contexts.

Given the demonstrated potency of autoethnography in generating changes through the dialogic discovery of self in relation to others and contexts, it is conceivable to design an autoethnographic model that shapes the transformative process to optimize the transformative outcome while simultaneously acknowledging that we do not have control over the trajectory of such outcomes. We call this the transformative autoethnography model (TAM). The TAM acknowledges the importance of the autoethnographic process that engenders consequential transformation but does not stop there. Instead, it harnesses the transformative energy of self-discovery from the autoethnographic process for purposeful transformation. The TAM positions purposeful transformation of self, others, and organization as the central intent of its inquiry efforts. This model will be discussed in detail in Chapter Four after autoethnographic methodology and cases—both individual and collaborative formats—are thoroughly discussed in Chapters Two and Three.

Summary

Autoethnography is an inquiry method that can be used for individual self-discovery as well as group-based collaborative endeavors. In this chapter, we identified six characteristics of autoethnography; it: (1) pursues an in-depth understanding of sociocultural phenomena as an inquiry method: (2) captures personal experiences through the power of storying; (3) utilizes autoethnographers' personal experiences as primary data; (4) offers the options of taking the interrogation individually or collaboratively; (5) engages the autoethnographic process for both research and praxis purposes; and (6) results in diverse forms of autoethnographic products.

In addition to these six key features, self-reflexivity and transformation are noted as inextricable elements of autoethnographic work. Self-reflexivity is defined as a deep and critical self-examination in relation to others to discover how the relational self is shaped within one's sociocultural contexts. Autoethnographic self-reflexivity engenders transformative consequences to oneself, to others with whom one is associated, and to the environment in which the individual resides. Transformation is defined as substantial and potentially sustainable change in cognitive, affective, psychological, spiritual, and/or behavioral domains of individuals, communities, and organizations. While affirming that the autoethnographic process has potential to generate such transformation and has demonstrated transformative power in the extant literature, we propose the transformative autoethnography model (TAM) to harness the transformative power of autoethnography in praxis applications.

References

Acosta, S., Goltz, H. H., & Goodson, P. (2015). Autoethnography in action research for health education practitioners. *Action research, 13*(4), 411–431. https://doi.org/10.1177/147675031 5573589

Adams, T. E. (2012). *Narrating the closet: An autoethnography of same-sex attraction.* Left Coast Press.

Adams, T. E., Ellis, C., & Holman Jones, S. (2014). *Autoethnography.* Oxford.

Adams, T. E., Holman Jones, S., & Ellis, C. (Eds.). (2021). *Handbook of autoethnography* (2nd ed.). Routledge.

Adams, T. E. & Manning, J. (2015). Autoethnography and family research. *Journal of Family Theory & Review, 8.* 350–366. DOI:10.1111/jftr.12116

Alexander, B. K., Moreira, C., & Kumar, H. S. (2015). Memory, mourning, and miracles: A triple-autoethnographic performance script. *International Review of Qualitative Research, 8*(2), 229–255. https://doi.org/10.1525/irqr.2015.8.2.229

Anderson, L. (2006). Analytic autoethnography. *Journal of Contemporary Ethnography, 35*(4), 373–395. https://doi.org/10.1177/0891241605280449

Atkinson, P. (2006). Rescuing autoethnography. *Journal of Contemporary Ethnography, 35*, 400–404. https://doi.org/10.1177/0891241606286980

Berger R. (2015). Now I see it, now I don't: Researcher's position and reflexivity in qualitative research. *Qualitative Research. 15*(2), 219–234. https://doi.org/10.1177/1468794112468475

Berry, K., Gillotti, C. M., & Adams, T. (2019). *Living sexuality: Stories of LGBTQ relationships, identities, and desires.* Brill.

Bhattacharya, K. (2018). Coloring memories and imaginations of "home": Crafting a de/colonizing autoethnography. *Cultural Studies↔Critical Methodologies, 18*(1), 9–15. https://doi.org/10.1177/1532708617734010

Blalock, A. E., & Akehi, M. (2018). Collaborative autoethnography as a pathway for transformative learning. *Journal of Transformative Education, 16*(2), 89–107. https://doi.org/10.1177/1541344617715711

Bochner, A. P. (2010). Resisting the mystification of narrative inquiry: Unmasking the real conflict between story analysts and storytellers. *Sociology of Health & Illness, 32*(4), 662–665, https://doi.org/10.1111/j.1467-9566.2010.01240_2.x

Bochner, A., & Ellis, C. (2016). *Evocative autoethnography: Writing lives and telling stories.* Routledge.

Boyle, M., & Parry, K. (2007). Telling the whole story: The case for organizational autoethnography. *Culture and Organization, 13*(3), 185–190.

Boylorn, R. M., & Orbe, M. P. (Eds.). (2020). *Critical autoethnography: Intersecting cultural identities in everyday life.* Routledge.

Canagarajah, A. S. (2012). Teacher development in a global profession: An autoethnography. *TESOL Quarterly, 46*(2), 258–279. https://doi.org/10.1002/tesq.18

Carless, D., & Douglas, K. (2021). Collaborative autoethnography: From rhythm and harmony to shared stories and truths. In T. E. Adams, S. Holman Jones, & C. Ellis (Eds.), *Handbook of autoethnography* (2nd ed, pp. 155–166). Routledge.

Chang, H. (2008). *Autoethnography as method*. Routledge.

Chang, H. (2013). Individual and collaborative autoethnography as method. In S. Holman Jones, T. E. Adams, & C. Ellis (Eds.), *Handbook of autoethnography* (pp. 107–122). Routledge.

Chang, H. (2016). Autoethnography in health research: Growing pains? *Qualitative health research, 26*(4), 443–451. https://doi.org/10.1177/1049732315627432

Chang, H. (2021). Individual and collaborative autoethnography for social science research. In T. E. Adams, S. Holman Jones, C. Ellis (Eds.), *Handbook of autoethnography* (2nd ed., pp. 53–66). Routledge.

Chang, H. (in press). Where the personal meets the sociocultural: Autoethnography for social science research, praxis, and pedagogy. In A. Porferl & N. Schröer (Eds.), *Handbuch sociologische ethnographie [Handbook of sociological ethnography]*. Springer-Verlag.

Chang, H., Longman, K. A., & Franco, M. A. (2014). Leadership development through mentoring in higher education: A collaborative autoethnography of leaders of color. *Mentoring & Tutoring: Partnership in Learning, 22*(4), 373–389. https://doi.org/10.1080/13611267.2014.9 45734

Chang, H., Ngunjiri, F. W., & Hernandez, K. C. (2013). *Collaborative autoethnography*. Routledge.

Coffey, A. (1999). *The ethnographic self*. London: SAGE.

Cormier, É. (2020). *The dying roles: A creative autoethnographic exploration of roles at the end of life*. [Unpublished manuscript.] Concordia University. Spectrum Research Repository. https:// spectrum.library.concordia.ca/id/eprint/986989/

Denzin, N. K. (2014). *Interpretive autoethnography* (2nd ed.). SAGE.

Denzin, N. K. (2018). *Performance autoethnography: Critical pedagogy and the politics of culture*. Routledge.

Denzin, N. K., & Lincoln, Y. S. (Eds.) (2005). *The SAGE handbook of qualitative research* (3rd ed.). SAGE.

Diversi, M., & Moreira, C. (2018). *Betweener autoethnographies: A path towards social justice*. Routledge.

Diversi, M., Gale, K., Moreira, C., & Wyatt, J. (2020). Writing with: Collaborative writing as hope and resistance. *International Review of Qualitative Research, 14*(2), 302–312. https://doi.org/10.1177/1940844720978761

Dunn, T. R. (2020). Divorce in the digital age: A cyber autoethnographic exploration. *International Review of Qualitative Research, 13*(3), 297–316. https://doi.org/10.1177/1940844720937816

Ellis, C. (1998). Interpretive ethnography: Ethnographic practices for the twenty-first century. *Contemporary Sociology, 27*(4), 422–424. https://doi.org/10.2307/2655524

Ellis, C. (2004). *The ethnographic I: A methodological novel about autoethnography*. Rowman Altamira.

Ellis, C., (2016). Preface: Carrying the torch for autoethnography. In S. Holman Jones, T. E. Adams & C. Ellis (Eds.), *Handbook of autoethnography* (pp. 9–12). Routledge.

Ellis, C., Adams, T. E., & Bochner, A. P. (2011). Autoethnography: an overview. *Historical social research/Historische sozialforschung*, 273–290. https://doi.org/10.17169/fqs-12.1.1589

Ellis, C., & Rawicki, J. (2013). Collaborative witnessing of survival during the Holocaust: An exemplar of relational autoethnography. *Qualitative Inquiry, 19*(5), 366–380. https://doi.org/10.1177/1077800413479562

Faulkner, S. L. (2017). Poetry is politics: An autoethnographic poetry manifesto. *International Review of Qualitative Research, 10*(1), 89–96. https://doi.org/10.1525/irqr.2017.10.1.89

Feucht, F. C., Lunn Brownlee, J., & Schraw, G. (2017). Moving beyond reflection: Reflexivity and epistemic cognition in teaching and teacher education. *Educational Psychologist, 52*(4), 234–241. https://doi.org/10.1080/00461520.2017.1350180

Fourie, I. (2021). Analytic autoethnography. In *Autoethnography for librarians and information scientists* (pp. 49–60). Routledge.

Frank, A. W. (2009). Why I wrote . . . the wounded storyteller: A recollection of life and ethics. *Clinical Ethics, 4*(2), 106–108. https://doi.org/10.1258/ce.2009.009014

Frank, A. W. (2000). The standpoint of storyteller. *Qualitative health research, 10*(3), 354–365. https://doi.org/10.1177/104973200129118499

Frank, A. W. (2010). In defence of narrative exceptionalism. *Sociology of Health & Illness, 32*(4), 665–667. https://doi.org/10.1111/j.1467-9566.2010.01240_3.x

Freire, P. (1970). *Pedagogy of the oppressed*. Herter and Herter.

Gale, K., & Wyatt, J. (2019). Autoethnography and activism: Movement, intensity, and potential. *Qualitative Inquiry, 25*(6), 566–568. https://doi.org/10.1177/1077800418800754

Glowacki-Dudka, M., Treff, M., & Usman, I. (2005). Research for social change: Using autoethnography to foster transformative learning. *Adult Learning, 16*(3/4), 30. https://doi.org/10.1177/104515950501600308

Gnanadass, E., Murray-Johnson, K., & Alicia Vetter, M. (2021). Narrating the immigrant experience: Three adult educators' perspectives. *Adult Learning, 32*(1), 40–49. https://doi.org/10.1177/1045159520977708

Habermas, J. (1984). *The theory of communicative action. Vol. 1: Reason and the rationalization of society* (T. McCarthy, Trans.). Beacon.

Hayno, D. (1979). Auto-ethnography: Paradigms, problems and prospects. *Human Organisation, 38*(1), 99–104. https://doi.org/10.17730/humo.38.1.u761n5601t4g318v

Hermans, H. J. (2001). The dialogical self: Toward a theory of personal and cultural positioning. *Culture & Psychology, 7*(3), 243–281. https://doi.org/10.1177/1354067X0173001

Hermans, H., & Hermans-Konopka, A. (2010). *Dialogical self theory: Positioning and counterpositioning in a globalizing society*. Cambridge University Press.

Hernandez, K. C. (2021). Collaborative autoethnography as method and praxis: understanding self and others in practice. In I. Fourie (Ed.), *Autoethnography for Librarians and Information Scientists* (pp. 61–76). Routledge.

Hernandez, K. C., Ngunjiri, F. W., & Chang, H. (2014). Exploiting the margins in higher education: A collaborative autoethnography of three foreign-born female faculty of color. *International Journal of Qualitative Studies in Education, 28*(5), 533–551. https://doi.org/10.1080/09518398.2014.933910

Herrmann, A. F. (Ed.). (2020). The Routledge international handbook of organizational autoethnography. Routledge.

Hoggan, C. D. (2016). Transformative learning as a metatheory: Definition, criteria, and typology. *Adult Education Quarterly, 66*(1), 57–75. https://doi.org/10.1177/0741713615611216

Holman Jones, S. (2005). Autoethnography: Making the personal political. In N. Denzin & Y. S. Lincoln (Eds.), *The SAGE handbook of qualitative research* (3rd ed., pp. 763–791). SAGE.

Holman Jones, S. (2008). Autoethnography: Making the personal political. In N. K. Denzin & Y. S. Lincoln (Eds.), *Collecting and interpreting qualitative materials* (3rd ed., pp. 205-245). Thousand Oaks, CA: Sage.

Holman Jones, S. (2018). Creative selves/creative cultures: Critical autoethnography, performance, and pedagogy. In *Creative selves/creative cultures* (pp. 3–20). Palgrave Macmillan.

Holman Jones, S., Adams, T. E., & Ellis, C. (Eds.). (2015). *The handbook of autoethnography*. Routledge.

Horton, M., & Friere, P. (1990). *We make the road by walking: Conversations on education and social change*. Temple University Press.

Hughes, S. A., & Pennington, J. L. (2016). *Autoethnography: Process, product, and possibility for critical social research*. SAGE.

Hunter, A. (2020). Snapshots of selfhood: Curating academic identity through visual autoethnography. *International Journal for Academic Development, 25*(4), 310–323. https://doi.org/1 0.1080/1360144X.2020.1755865

Jensen-Hart, S., & Williams, D. J. (2010). Blending voices: Autoethnography as a vehicle for critical reflection in social work. *Journal of Teaching in Social Work, 30*(4), 450–467. https:// doi.org/10.1080/08841233.2010.515911

Keating, A., & González-López, G. (2011). *Bridging: How Gloria Anzaldúa's life and work transformed our own*. Austin: University of Texas Press.

Kegan, R. (2018). What "form" transforms?: A constructive-developmental approach to transformative learning. In K. Illeris (Ed.), *Contemporary theories of learning* (2nd ed., pp. 29–45). Routledge.

Kegan, R. (2000). What "form" transforms? A constructive-developmental approach to transformative learning. In J. Mezirow & Associates (Eds.), *Learning as transformation: Critical perspectives on a theory in progress* (pp. 35–70). Jossey-Bass.

Kiesinger, C. E. (2002). My father's shoes: The therapeutic value of narrative reframing. In A.P. Bochner & C. Ellis (Eds.). (2002). *Ethnographically speaking: Autoethnography, literature, and aesthetics* (Vol. 9, pp. 95–114). Rowman Altamira.

Kniffin, L. E., Van Schyndel, T., Fornaro, E. G., Purcell, J. W., & Muse, S. (2021). Next generation practitioner-scholars navigating community engagement professional development: A collaborative autoethnography. *Journal of Community Engagement and Higher Education, 13*(1), 57–77. https://files.eric.ed.gov/fulltext/EJ1294684.pdf

Koopman, W. J., Watling, C. J., & LaDonna, K. A. (2020). Autoethnography as a strategy for engaging in reflexivity. *Global Qualitative Nursing Research, 7*. https://doi.org/10.1177/2333 393620970508

Kuhn, T. (1962). *The structure of scientific revolutions*. University of Chicago Press.

Longman, K. A., Chang, H., & Loyd-Paige, M. (2015). Self-analytical, community-building, and empowering: Collaborative autoethnography of leaders of color in higher education. *Journal of Ethnographic & Qualitative Research, 9*(4). 268–285.

López, C. J., & Tracy, S. J. (2020). Anchoring "the big tent": How organizational autoethnography exemplifies and stretches notions of qualitative quality. In A. F. Herman (Ed.)., *The Routledge International Handbook of Organizational Autoethnography* (pp. 383–398). Routledge.

MacGregor Burns, J. (2003). *Transforming leadership: The pursuit of happiness.* The Atlantic Monthly Press.

McIlveen, P. (2008). Autoethnography as a method for reflexive research and practice in vocational psychology. *Australian Journal of Career Development, 17*(2), 13–20. https://doi.org/1 0.1177/103841620801700204

McPhail-Bell, K., & Redman-MacLaren, M. (2019). A co/autoethnography of peer support and PhDs: Being, doing, and sharing in academia. *The Qualitative Report, 24*(5), 1087–1105. https://doi.org/10.46743/2160-3715/2019.3155

Mezirow, J. (1991). *Transformative dimensions in adult learning.* Jossey-Bass.

Mezirow, J. (1997). Transformative learning: Theory to practice. In P. Cranton (Ed.), *Transformative learning in action: Insights from practice* (New Directions for Adult and Continuing Education, no. 74, pp. 5–12). Jossey-Bass.

Mezirow, J. (2000). Learning to think like an adult: Core concepts of transformation theory. In *Learning as transformation: Critical perspectives on a theory in progress* (The Jossey-Bass Higher and Adult Education Series, 3-33). Jossey-Bass.

Mezirow, J. & Associates. (1990). *Fostering critical reflection in adulthood: A guide to transformative and emancipatory learning.* Jossey-Bass.

Moreira, C. (2011). (Un) Safe! Fighting the po-lice in quasi-educational spaces of bathrooms: A betweener's reflection on the researcher's body in three intercalated acts. *Cultural Studies? Critical Methodologies, 11*(2), 145–152. https://doi.org/10.1177/1532708611401333

Ngunjiri, F. W., Chang, H, & Hernandez, K. C. (2017). Multivocal meaning making: Using collaborative autoethnography to advance theory on women and leadership. In P. Haber-Curran P. & J. Stroberg-Walker (Eds.) *Theorizing women and leadership: New insights and contributions from multiple perspectives.* (pp. 103–119). Information Age Press.

Ngunjiri, F. W., Hernandez, K. C., & Chang, H. (2010). Living autoethnography: Connecting life and research. *Journal of Research Practice, 6*(1), E1-E1.

Norwood, C. R. (2018). Decolonizing my hair, unshackling my curls: An autoethnography on what makes my natural hair journey a Black feminist statement. *International Feminist Journal of Politics, 20*(1), 69–84. https://doi.org/10.1080/14616742.2017.1369890

Nowakowski, A. C., & Sumerau, J. E. (2019). Reframing health and illness: A collaborative autoethnography on the experience of health and illness transformations in the life course. *Sociology of Health & Illness, 41*(4), 723–739. https://doi.org/10.1111/1467-9566.12849

O'Connell, L. (2021). Being and doing anorexia nervosa: An autoethnography of diagnostic identity and performance of illness. *Health.* https://doi.org/10.1177/13634593211017190

O'Neil, S. M. (2018). On becoming a better supervisor: A deconstruction of autoethnography as method for professional development. *South African Journal of Higher Education, 32*(6), 483–501. https://doi.org/10.20853/32-6-2970

Oswald, A. G., Bussey, S., Thompson, M., & Ortega-Williams, A. (2020). Disrupting hegemony in social work doctoral education and research: Using autoethnography to uncover possibilities for radical transformation. *Qualitative Social Work,* https://doi.org/10.1177/1473325020973342

Pinner, R. S. (2018). Re-learning from experience: Using autoethnography for teacher development. *Educational Action Research, 26*(1), 91–105. https://doi.org/10.1080/09650792.2017.1 310665

Ploder, A., & Stadlbauer, J. (2016). Strong reflexivity and its critics: Responses to autoethnography in the German-speaking cultural and social sciences. *Qualitative Inquiry, 22*(9), 753–765. https://doi.org/10.1177/1077800416658067

Poplin, M. (2011). Finding Calcutta: Confronting secular imperative. In H. Chang & D. Boyd (Eds.), *Spirituality in higher education: Autoethnographies* (pp. 51–68). Routledge.

Poulos, C. N. (2019). Stand up! A performance autoethnography of resistance. *Qualitative Inquiry, 25*(6), 547–549. https://doi.org/10.1177/1077800418806611

Poulos, C. N. (2020). The perils and the promises of autoethnography: Raising our voices in troubled times. *Journal of Autoethnography, 1*(2), 208–211. https://doi.org/10.1525/joae.2020.1.2.208

Poulos, C. N. (2021). *Essentials of autoethnography*. American Psychological Association.

Preston, C., & Fraser-Thomas, J. (2018). Problematizing the pursuit of personal development and performance success: An autoethnography of a Canadian elite youth ice hockey coach. *The Sport Psychologist, 32*(2), 102–113. https://doi.org/10.1123/tsp.2016-0099

Ramírez-Pereira, M., Espinoza-Lobos, M., & Zapata-Sepúlveda, P. (2018). Interpretive autoethnography as a way of social transformation in academic teaching and learning spaces in Chile. *Cultural Studies↔Critical Methodologies, 18*(2), 99–106. https://doi.org/10.1177/1532708616657099

Reed-Danahay, D. (2017). Bourdieu and critical autoethnography: Implications for research, writing, and teaching. *International Journal of Multicultural Education, 19*(1), 144–154. https://doi.org/10.18251/ijme.v19i1.1368

Reed-Danahay, D. (Ed.). (2021). *Auto/ethnography: Rewriting the self and the social*. Routledge. (Original work published 1997)

Ross, S. L. (2020). A concept analysis of the form that trans-forms as a result of transformation. *International Journal of Psychological Studies, 12*(2), 52. https://doi.org/10.5539/ijps.v12n2p52

Sambrook, S., & Herrmann, A. F. (2018). Organisational autoethnography: Possibilities, politics and pitfalls. *Journal of Organizational Ethnography, 7*(3), 222–234. https://doi.org/10.1108/JOE-10-2018-075

Scarles, C. (2010). Where words fail, visuals ignite: Opportunities for visual autoethnography in tourism research. *Annals of Tourism Research, 37*(4), 905–926. https://doi.org/10.1016/j.annals.2010.02.001

Schapiro, S. A., Gallegos, P. V., Stashower, K., & Clark, D. F. (2017). Reflections on the 12th international transformative learning conference: Engaging at the intersections of theory and practice. *Journal of Transformative Education, 15*(1), 6–15. https://doi.org/10.1177/1541344616685644

Shepherd, J., Laven, D., & Shamma, L. (2020). Autoethnographic journeys through contested spaces. *Annals of Tourism Research, 84*, 103004. https://doi.org/10.1016/j.annals.2020.103004

Short, N. P., Turner, L., & Grant, A. (Eds.). (2013). *Contemporary British autoethnography*. Springer Science & Business Media.

Spry, T. (2001). Performing autoethnography: An embodied methodological praxis. *Qualitative Inquiry, 7*(6), 706–732. https://doi.org/10.1177/107780040100700605

Spry, T. (2017). Who are "we" in performative autoethnography? *International Review of Qualitative Research, 10*(1), 46–53. https://doi.org/10.1525/irqr.2017.10.1.46

Stahlke Wall, S. (2016). Toward a moderate autoethnography. *International Journal of Qualitative Methods, 15*(1). https://doi.org/10.1177/1609406916674966

Sykes, B. E. (2014). Transformative autoethnography: An examination of cultural identity and its implications for learners. *Adult Learning, 25*(1), 3–10. https://doi.org/10.1177/10451595 13510147

Taylor, J. Y., Mackin, M. A. L., & Oldenburg, A. M. (2008). Engaging racial autoethnography as a teaching tool for womanist inquiry. *Advances in Nursing Science, 31*(4), 342–355. https://doi. org/10.1097/01.ANS.0000341414.03963.fa

Tillmann, L. (2009). Body and bulimia revisited: Reflections on "A Secret Life." *Journal of Applied Communication Research – Journal of Applied Communication Research 37*, 98–112. https:// doi.org/10.1080/00909880802592615.

Tisdell, E. J. (2012). Themes and variations in transformational learning: Interdisciplinary perspective on forms that transform. In E.W. Taylor, P. Cranton, and Associates (Eds.), *The handbook of transformative learning: Theory, research, and practice* (pp. 21–36). John Wiley and Sons.

Turner, L., Short, N. P., Grant, A., & Adams, T. E. (Eds.). (2018). *International perspectives on autoethnographic research and practice.* Routledge.

Walford, G. (2004). Finding the limits: Autoethnography and being an Oxford University proctor. *Qualitative research, 4*(3), 403–417. https://doi.org/10.1177/1468794104047238

Whalen, G. C., & Simmons, T. E. (2021). Bonded from brokenness: A collaborative autoethnography on maternal bereavement. *Illness, Crisis & Loss.* https://doi.org/10.1177/1054137 320988476

Wiesner, A. (2020). Contemplating reflexivity as a practice of authenticity in autoethnographic research. *The Qualitative Report, 25*(3), 662–670. https://doi.org/10.46743/2160-3715/2020.3679

Yarborough, J. P., & Lowe, K. B. (2007). Unlocking foreclosed beliefs: An autoethnographic story about a family business leadership dilemma. *Culture and Organization, 13*(3), 239–249. https://doi.org/10.1080/14759550701486597

Zawadzki, M., & Jensen, T. (2020). Bullying and the neoliberal university: A coauthored autoethnography. *Management Learning, 51*(4), 398–413. https://doi.org/10.1177/1350507620920532

Zou, T. X. P., Law, L. Y. N., Chu, B. C. B., Lin, V., Ko, T., & Lai, N. K. Y. (2020). Developing academics' capacity for internationalizing the curriculum: A collaborative autoethnography of a cross-institutional project. *Journal of Studies in International Education.* https://doi.org/ 10.1177/1028315320976040

TWO

Individual Autoethnography (IAE) for Transformation

Wendy's Story

W HEN I DECIDED TO CONDUCT an autoethnographic study for my dissertation research, personal transformation was at most a side effect that I was anticipating. As a seasoned social worker and an incurable idealist, I wanted to change the world, not necessarily change myself. In spite of knowing how language and stories shape experience, and that all social work change processes begin with a person-in-environment interaction, my focus was on changing something out there and apart from me. Ironically, by the end of my autoethnographic exploration, I was the one who had changed, but I was not so sure about the world.

I had chosen as the focus of my dissertation an exploration of my own leadership identity construction, with an eye toward the impact of religious influences in my life. It was something I felt compelled to undertake, and based on the literature, it seemed like a personal journey that few leaders were taking. Perhaps my own exploration and laying bare of my leadership identity journey would show a path that others would be inspired to take? Maybe such an exploration would provide meaningful insights for the common good? At least that was my thinking. I was looking forward to a deep level of self-other-society examination and what I would learn. However, I was taken aback by the way the research process "laid bare many aspects of myself as well as many cultural assumptions of which I was blissfully ignorant." Truth be told, "the research process expanded me, aged me, and matured me as a researcher and leader" (Bilgen, 2018, p. 232) in ways that exceeded my original expectations.

By the end of my autoethnographic dissertation, I had faced many things about myself and society and was better equipped to invite others on transformative journeys with me. Doing autoethnography changed me, but is that the same as saying autoethnography was transformative for me? And if it was transformative, how could this be stretched beyond myself and into the world? Working on this book has helped me grapple with these lingering questions.

****

As we described in the previous chapter, transformative experiences are understood and identified in various ways. But what is it that *transforms (does the transforming?)* in autoethnography? What mechanism of transformation does individual autoethnography engage that results in multilevel (individual, community, organizational, societal), ongoing, substantial change in knowledge, insights, and/or behaviors?

Self-reflexivity, as described in Chapter One, uniquely positions the individual autoethnographer for multiple forms of transformation. In fact, proponents of transformative practice highlight the role of critical reflection on one's past experiences and assumptions as a precursor to any form of transformation (Tisdell, 2012). Because autoethnography is dependent on the self-reflexive processes that lead to transformation, it does not surprise us that transformative outcomes are common among autoethnographers. The self-reflexive processes unique to autoethnography are often *therapeutic, healing, affirming, empowering, redemptive, transformative.* These words were shared among autoethnographers during a virtual session of the 2021 International Symposium on Autoethnography and Narrative as attendees reflected on the impact of both producing their own and experiencing autoethnographic works of others.

These descriptions match our own experiences both interacting with and producing autoethnography over the years. Autoethnography has the capacity to change people, and as people change, so too do their relationships, their communities, and their societies. But still the question remains: What is it about autoethnography that stimulates transformative change? We considered transformation in relation to autoethnographic work generally in our previous chapter. Now we turn our attention to the transformative processes and outcomes specific to individual autoethnography.

Individual Autoethnography Methodology

Individual autoethnography (IAE) starts with an individual's desire to explore issues that are close to a researcher's heart. Curiosity around a life-changing, peak, or traumatic experience captures the attention of the researcher and motivates the embodied, holistic, critical, and self-reflexive analysis and meaning-making of one's personal experiences that are the essence of the autoethnographic *process*. It is through critical self-exploration of our embodied experiences, using our whole self (engaging our mind, body, emotion, spirit) that transformative learning outcomes are thought to be most profound (Ross, 2020; Schapiro et al., 2017).

Transformation happens as the autoethnographer enlists creative forms of expression to uncover and then communicate their discoveries beyond the level of the intellect, and in a way that is felt in the body, in the emotions, and in the spirit. While autoethnography is certainly related to writing (the *-graphy* part of the word), autoethnographic work is also performative in that it presents and represents everyday emotionally charged lived experiences, wholistic events involving bodily movement as well as intellectual, emotional, and creative processes performed at the interface between the individual, the social environment, and society as a whole (Conquergood, 2002; Denzin, 2018; Pelias, 2010; Spry, 2011).

The individual autoethnographic *product* can also be considered a transformative feature of autoethnography. Because the autoethnographic tradition invites multiple expressions of one's story, the IAE product can be experienced through colorful, poetic, graphic descriptions, intense and realistic dialogue, and gripping metaphor. There is quite a different impact between sharing information and sharing one's experiences with detail, creativity, and art. Sharing information doesn't necessarily land in the whole body in the same way someone's graphic experiences might be "felt" through sensory images and descriptions capable of transferring you into the story of another.

Creative autoethnographic writing and other artistic presentations of one's work have helped to stretch the once-firm boundaries between science and art (Reed-Danahay, 1997/2021). By weaving together one's creative and academic voice, the autoethnographer is able to "fuse abstract theory with practical, lived circumstance" (Adams, 2012, p. 35) in a liberated, embodied, more authentic self-story. The autoethnographic product is often the story of a recovered or newly discovered voice, full of the creativity and artistry that evokes a response in others as art often does (Leavy, 2020).

Autoethnography, which was once considered boundary-pushing and destabilizing because of its unconventional style, has appealed to a whole new group of researchers and practitioners who had felt silenced by the limitations within the social sciences on what can be said and how (Denzin, 2018; Sparkes, 2018; Spry, 2011). At the same time, an emphasis on creativity and artful products means autoethnography appeals to a larger audience beyond the academy, increasing the transformative possibilities exponentially.

While artistic freedom within the autoethnographic tradition gives a freer space for individual expressive form, an equal concern for data collection, analysis, and sociocultural interpretation of lived experiences remains in the work (Stahlke Wall, 2016). Although processes and products may vary greatly, good autoethnographic work will harness the power of a single story, rely on dialogical interactions between the author and others, and be driven by a desire to discover truth and deepen understanding that ultimately results in an outcome that is transformative (Witkin, 2014). Now a brief look at how each of these components of autoethnography adds to the transformative possibilities.

Power of the Self Story

Autoethnography links our human drive for narrative structure to our human need for individual and collective meaning-making (Bruner, 2004; Denzin, 2014; Holman Jones et al., 2016; Leavy, 2020). In individual autoethnography, the story that emerges surrounds one participant's experience—the author's. The centering of the self as a single participant in research stands in contrast to past norms of qualitative research in which the aim was to understand the story of others. Instead of detached observations and interpretations of *other* worlds, individual autoethnographers "position themselves as initiators, subjects, and objects of their self-exploration" (Chang & Bilgen, 2020, p. 94).

Telling one's own story in autoethnographic research creates the space for attention to the physical, cognitive, emotional, and spiritual experiences that are seldom invited into research spaces. As popular speaker Brené Brown (2012) said in her now famous TED talk, our stories are data with souls. An individual autoethnographer attends to the particulars of their own story as unique data, driven by awareness that their story holds some insight around a particular human experience—which may be conflictual, damaging, confusing, oppressive, and painful—and that others in the world will likely relate. The initial awareness that something is troubling in one's story can be likened to the disorienting dilemma thought to be the first step in a journey of transformative learning (Mezirow & Associates, 1990). With awareness as the starting point, attention to one's experiences through autoethnographic processes can transform how we think (a change of mind), how we behave (a change in our bodies and how we move), how we feel with and empathize with others (a change in heart or soul), and how we understand our purpose in the world (a change in understanding the human connection and the common good). As researchers grapple openly with the grueling realities in their own lives and in the worlds they inhabit, sometimes speaking the unspeakable, they help to demystify and destigmatize struggles that are common to everyone. They do this primarily through self-narrative.

Autoethnographers privilege the personal view of self, grounded in the belief that individuals are uniquely positioned to make meaning of their own stories. Using privileged insider knowledge to probe highly personal, metaphysical, and political questions of greatest interest to them, individuals are free to say out loud that which has been unexamined—perhaps silenced by trauma, marginalized by power structures in society, or simply forbidden by social taboo or because some voices have not been invited to weigh in on certain topics (Boylorn & Orbe, 2020). The voice that is heard through autoethnographic telling is that of the author, uniquely speaking of what was uncovered, felt, named, and renamed, interrogated, and changed within the self, but hoping to stimulate the same in others and in society.

The storying process, much like a therapy process, adds needed coherence and meaning-making to what are experienced as disorienting and traumatic events in the life of the autoethnographer. Through the use of language and symbols, performed in the presence of others who bear witness to the experience, links are made between ideas and experiences lived in a sequence across time and according to a plot; from new discoveries, the autoethnographer shapes a new story. And so storytellers transform their own "experiential 'chaos' into coherent and decipherable forms" (Frank, 2013, p. 166). Again, language shapes experience. Through retold, restructured, transformed stories, autoethnograpers can take themselves and others into new life experiences.

Dialogicality

Even though the author is the sole subject of individual autoethnography, autoethnographic processes are foregrounded in *dialogicality*. That is, the researcher seeks to understand their own reality as a construct highly dependent on others in their social environment and through social interactions. In this way, the autoethnographic "I" is understood to be a "plural pronoun" (Spry, 2011, p. 94). Figure 2.1 shows the levels of interaction that takes place between the individual autoethnographer and related others.

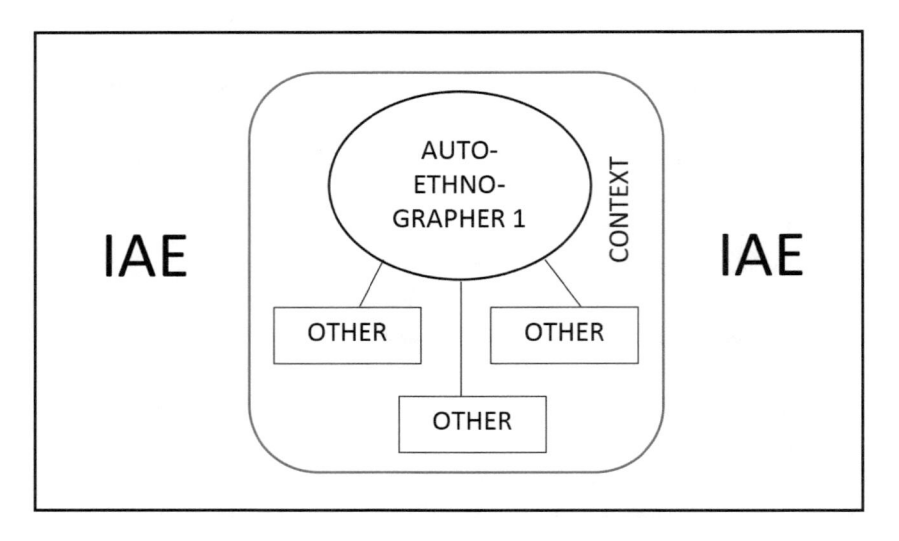

Figure 2.1. Individual Autoethnography (IAE)

In IAE, there is an acknowledged reciprocal influence between the researcher, the setting, and other participants, including the eventual readers, which all lead to the cocreation of knowledge and the potential for change (Anderson & Glass-Coffin, 2013).

Thus the autoethnographic story first speaks about and to the author, but ultimately speaks to others, creating and utilizing "critical spaces for dialogical, interrelational, and intersectional exchanges to be made between the storyteller/storymaker, her lived and embodied experiences, and the readers" (Metta, 2013, p. 494). And so it is a plural I that stimulates new and profound insights into a single case. This dialogical feature of autoethnography celebrates human interconnectivity, that an individual struggle is always interwoven with communal activity and set in larger social and political structures. Dialogical interaction occurs with others through scholarly literature, interactive interviewing, and other dialogue with one's colleagues, family members, and a whole community of others.

Generally, autoethnographers are also eager for others to connect with their stories in a holistic way. As Ellis and Bochner (2017) put it, autoethnographers want "you to interact with their stories, using all the senses available to you, feeling each story's tensions, experiencing their dilemmas or contradictions, and living in the reality of the story for a time" (p. vii.). The story can become a cocreated experience between the autoethnographer and the audience who is invited as a participant in the autoethnographic change experience. The autoethnographer as storyteller invites others to help them see their world and experiences from a wider angle. The perspective change that is key to transformative learning has an opportunity to grow in the space between the self and the other (Mezirow & Associates, 1990).

A series of dialogical encounters occurs throughout the IAE process as the autoethnographer engages others in interactive interviewing and other forms of self/other examination with the intention to bring something to light that, without the insight of another viewpoint, would go unnoticed, unchallenged, unexamined, and unchanged (Denzin, 2003). Harkening back to the notion that our self stories are always performed in the community of others, Denzin (2003) remarked that "the autoethnographer invites members of the community to become co-performers in a drama of social resistance and social critique . . . offering emotional support to one another, coperformers bear witness to the need for social change" (p. 17). In this way, the dialogical process in IAE is multidirectional, having the capacity to evoke changes in the researcher, those who are part of the researcher's investigation, and those who are the readers/audience.

Self-Discovery and Deep Understanding

As one attempts to make meaning of personal experiences through reciprocal and dialogical relationship to others, the conclusions reached are *true* only for the author. Still, autoethnographers continually reposition themselves with one eye on the *truths* they discovered about themselves and within their own story, and another eye on sociological, cultural, and political analysis that suggests larger *truths* that can be applied to others. The aim then is to share discoveries that will inevitably connect with some others, but perhaps in very different ways than what the author intended.

Finding a single generalizable truth is not the purpose of autoethnography (Ellis, 2004). Rather, naturalistic generalizations will occur in which readers might compare their own everyday life experiences to the rich, detailed, sensory accounts provided by the author's narrative (Melrose, 2010). Transformative experiences can occur for the individual autoethnographer as the author questions their own situated experiences, welcomes the disruptions to self and social context that such scrutiny brings, and invites the deconstruction and reconstruction of "taken for granted master narratives about how life is or is supposed to be" (Short et al., 2013, p. 4). Autoethnography fulfills the function of giving space for once-marginalized voices to speak their truths, shaping individual lives in healing and meaning-filled ways, and stimulating social change (Witkin, 2014).

In sum, the possibilities for self-discovery and deep understanding exist for the autoethnographer and the many others involved in the process and product of IAE. First, the author comes to a deeper understanding of self through the storying process. Then, in an act that has been described as "a generosity of spirit," the author shares the IAE product with others as a means of invitation for connection, to "feel with others, to understand what others see" (Pelias, 1999, p. xiii). Some may take advantage of this opportunity to connect to the author's experience by comparing their own everyday lived experiences to the accounts provided by the author's narrative. Yet what provokes transformation in the author may differ from what is evoked in the reader by the author's story. The IAE journey in self-discovery and understanding is primarily a personal change journey, but it is not "insular" or "singular." Rather it is a "dialogical invitation" into the power of stories that speaks to multiple audiences, and "from which others can learn and grow" (Berry & Patti, 2015, p. 266).

Transformative Dimensions in Individual Autoethnography

One might be left questioning, "Is individual autoethnography primarily therapeutic, healing, confrontational, political?" The answer is yes; it is all those things, and perhaps even more. As explored in our introductory chapter, transformative processes and outcomes are conceptualized and experienced in many ways. We consider that transformation might be evident at three distinct levels: individually (micro level, internal changes), relationally (meso level, our connections to others), and socially (macro level, addressing power structures in society). Transformative experiences, whether in therapy, in the classroom, through family and work encounters, or in autoethnographic research, occur at multiple levels.

Discoveries through autoethnographic inquiry might begin at the cognitive level, but deepen through embodied experience, dialogic encounters, emotional engagement, and finally narratively structuring (or *storying*). Exploration of one's narratively structured experiences becomes fertile ground for further change processes to flourish. While these processes begin at the individual level, they inevitably ripple into the relationships we have with others, and into the larger social contexts in which we live. Each level of transformation (individual, relational, societal) will be looked at separately with examples of each type, illustrating the diverse and far-reaching transformative possibilities that all begin with an author's curiosity around their own embodied experiences.

Therapeutic Healing

While autoethnographic practice was not developed specifically as a method for healing emotional experiences, narrating one's experiences through intentional self-reflexive processes often results in therapeutic outcomes for the individual authethnographer (Frank, 2013; Grant, 2010; Herrmann, 2016; Lengelle 2021; Speedy, 2013). The Greek word for therapy (*therapeutikos*) literally means *to attend to*. It implies that as we attend to the emotion accompanying the details of our lives, organizing and making meaning of life events, we can naturally expect a therapeutic or healing impact. In *The Wounded Storyteller*, Arthur Frank (2013), suggests that illness, emotional pain, and trauma wounds lodge "not just in body but in voice" (p. 7) or in the ability or lack of ability to tell our story. One can therefore expect therapeutic healing to occur as storytellers "recover their voice" (p. 9) and find words for previously unexpressed emotion and meaning from challenging experiences that once were chaotic.

The narrative processes that unfold through storytelling in autoethnography mirror the therapeutic narrative structuring approach developed by White and Epston (1990) in their classic work *Narrative Means to Therapeutic Ends*. In this therapeutic approach, individuals explore the particulars of their experiences attending to body, emotion, setting, other characters, dialogue, plot, and crisis, noticing new sensations, emotions, and epiphanies. The narrative therapist helps their clients make meaning of their experiences as together they craft a new story about past experiences. Søren Kierkegaard's sentiment that life is understood backwards, but must be lived forward (Kirsch, 2020), guides the practice of narrative storytelling in therapy. The therapeutic impact of storytelling arises from the ability to narratively structure one's life experiences, taking something that has not been fully articulated, bringing it into full view to be felt, analyzed, questioned, challenged, and understood in a new way, provoking new understanding and new behavior (McIlveen, 2008; White & Epston, 1990). In therapy, transformation is seen as individuals put words to experiences, which in turn gives new meaning to experiences.

There are many examples of therapeutic outcomes through autoethnographic exploration of illness, trauma, and loss. Perhaps it was Carolyn Ellis's (1995) groundbreaking autoethnographic work *Final Negotiations* that opened the way for an outpouring of autoethnographic writing around individual experiences with illness, death, and dying. Ellis turned to IAE to story her experiences dealing with the chronic illness and eventual death of her partner Gene. She used vulnerable, evocative, and often heart-wrenching descriptions, leaving the reader not only *knowing* more about the disease process but *feeling* the relationship impact, the grief cycle, and the ongoing negotiations with sorrow and loss that are embedded in her experience. In a later revision of *Final Negotiations* (2018), she directly addressed the personal transformative experience of being "an ethnographer of my own experience," noting that the "text that I constructed . . . in turn, constructed me" (p. 9).

Many autoethnographers have followed the lead of Ellis documenting their transformative experiences of illness and loss, creating insider accounts and inviting readers to bear witness to loss, even to become a fellow sufferer through empathic connection to their stories (Culkin, 2019; Lengelle, 2021; Tisdell, 2017). In Lengelle's (2021) *Writing the Self in Bereavement: A Story of Love, Spousal Loss, and Resilience*, she describes illness, death, and her own pathway through grief, and leaves the reader not only *feeling for*, but *feeling with*. Using poetry, imaginative dialogue, and sharing letters between herself and others grieving loss, it is clear that the author's IAE was a therapeutic endeavor for her. At the same time, her vulnerability opens the way for readers to feel with her, to bear witness to her loss, and perhaps carry their own loss in a way that was previously not imagined. Matthews (2019) also confirms the value of narrating loss in her account of "writing through grief" (p. 1) after tragically and suddenly losing her son. She wrote, "Autoethnography became an invaluable starting point for me to emotionally relocate and begin living a productive life again" (p. 8). Through the process of storying traumatic life events, individuals proactively take steps forward on the journey to healing.

Beyond empathic connection, narratives can give voice, or agency, to those who have felt marginalized because of their illness, loss, and trauma experience. Autoethnographic writing is an emancipatory practice; it is neither "innocent, nor is it passive . . . rather it is interested, and action in the world, an exercise of power" (Colyar, 2015, p. 373). Richards (2019) engaged in this emancipatory practice by narrating her experiences of feeling silenced by the shame and stigma of being a person "with a nonconforming body" (p. 271) in academia. The emancipatory discourse in autoethnography gave voice to the voicelessness Richards experienced, as writing enabled her to speak back to "dominant discourse that favours invulnerability and a masculinised, disembodied way of being academic" as she called out the "institutional tropes" (p. 270) around disability that are embedded within academia. We see another example of the emancipatory discourse in the work of Ferdinand (2018), who chose to tell her story "that would otherwise go unnoticed or unexamined" (p. 1576). Her description of being a Black woman diagnosed with lupus, continuously wrestling with the "larger critical issues of race, gender, and the social barriers to health care" (p. 1566) reveals personal resilience building in her through storytelling. Likewise O'Shea's (2019) self-described "emotive, and at times, visceral account of two aspects of my life as a nonbinary transgender person in transition and dysphoria" (p. 38) is intended to challenge the tropes in existing medical narratives as well as catalyze a vision something better for other transsexual folks navigating unwieldy healthcare systems. Such narratives are capable of destabilizing harmful norms around what it means to be normal, healthy, ill, or disabled (O'Shea, 2019; Richards, 2008).

Depictions such as these of complex loss and trauma reveal insight about specific cases, but also make wider claims about loss, the nature of trauma, survival, and the mechanisms in society that either help or hinder human flourishing. In a rare example of autoethnography by a prisoner speaking while serving a life sentence in prison, Mickelthwaite (Mickelthwaite & Earle, 2021) offers an insider perspective into how "challenges are negotiated in both prisoner culture and administrative procedures" (p. 2). Readers are also given a story of "private troubles" that address "public issues" (p. 4) of importance, but that are often not told from the perspective of the prisoner. Mickelthwaite shared a compelling story of his own suffering and growing resilience, sense of self-determination through productivity, connection to community, and ability to structure his daily life even when much of his self-determination was compromised by incarceration. His personal transformative story, done initially for his own sense-making, offers insight and coping strategies to others within and outside of the justice system. We see in these examples and others the transformative possibilities for self-healing increasing exponentially when narrating the self takes place in the presence of another person, one who can bear witness to, empathize with, and be enlightened by the experience of the storyteller.

Shaping Relational Identity and Behaviors

Psychologist Jerome Bruner (1985) once observed that the "self" is always also found in the "other" (p. 66). As such, our various relationships shape our identity and our behavior in the world. Individual narratives inevitably highlight relational experiences within the writer's own family, between professional and academic colleagues, romantic partners, and siblings, to name a few. Autoethnographic accounts address relational strain, ambivalence with identity, and threats to individuality, belonging, and connection that occur in individuals navigating increasingly complex social situations. Many autoethnographic accounts have helped to shed light and transform ideas about family roles, belonging, and relational dynamics (Adams, 2021), between teacher and student (Henderson, 2019), child and parent (Hannon, 2017; Herrmann 2016), perpetrator and victim (Javaid, 2020), individuals and organizations (Lengelle, 2016; O'Shea, 2019), therapist and client (Wyatt, 2021), the abused and abuser (Gildea, 2021), even God and worshipper (Gerena, 2019; Tisdell, 2017). These are but a few examples.

Personal stories that necessarily involve the stories of others will no doubt have an impact on the self as well as on the relational spaces in which individuals exist. For example, Moffitt's (2020) probe of the dynamics between herself and her daughter helped her interrogate her role as a Black mother in a racist world. As Moffitt recounted her daughter's realization that "you're brown Mommy, but light-skinned and I am brown, but dark-skinned" (p. 67), Moffit laments how unprepared she was for colorism to invade their relational world and how she navigated these societal intrusions. Likewise, Henderson (2019) shared her journey traversing the emotional and social landscape at the intersections of her multiple professional and familial roles of teacher and protector of other people's children, while also being mother and protector of her own children in an increasingly violent world. While all readers need not necessarily have experienced the effects of colorism or the fear-filled intricacies of working for child protection services, the stories compel considerations about self-esteem, race, identity, and the power of language to shape and change the stories we live in relationship with others.

Autoethnographies also often unravel complexities of intersecting dimensions of personal identity in relation to the social structures in society. Membership in particular social spaces sometimes creates the disorienting dilemmas related to *belonging* and/or *exclusion* as various identities intersect. The strain of overlapping identities feature as central themes in autoethnographic stories as individual autoethnographers wrestle with multiple and conflicting expectations and outcomes within their various roles and social contexts. For example Hannon's (2017) autoethnography revealed intrapersonal and interpersonal dilemmas of navigating being a Black father with an autistic son, attempting to present himself and his family as "middle-class, college educated, heterosexual, married, two-parent household" so that he might be seen as "respectable to our son's school district." (p. 155). Hannon's identity narrative helped him answer the question "Who am I?" and, more specifically, what does it mean to be *me* in a particular space and time, and in relationship to others. Through his story, he is able to take the reader along on his journey toward new understandings of social and relational realities that may otherwise remain unexamined.

As autoethnographers examine the intricacies of personal identity (based on inherent physical and psychological characteristics) and social identity (based on social roles and group membership), they uncover for themselves and reveal to others the many ways that multiple overlapping identities are conceived, experienced, and evolve over time and in challenging settings. An example is Villanueva's (2020) inner negotiation of multiple selves done while critiquing the politics of urban planning. In his autoethnographic "letter to his multiple selves," readers are invited to bear witness to his conversations with his own multiple voices of "community activist, urban planning practitioner, and scholar collaborating with marginalized communities of color in cities" (p. 157). From the position of a Filipino city planner, he is able to tell a unique story of participating in the gentrification of his own city neighborhood and the sense of complicity to injustice he experienced as a member of both groups. Through the text, the reader can witness the transformative processes in Villanova as he related in new ways to his own ethnic community, prompting him to give up the city planning entirely and become an advocate against gentrification.

Transformative learning is bound to occur as critical engagement with otherness opens new realities. Increased awareness of how our social identities position us as *the powerful* or *the powerless* in particular social contexts can lead to greater openness to others who are marginalized in our own spheres of life. And as global movement has become more and more common, we see many autoethnographers examining their experiences with multiple identities in cross cultural settings. Eguchi (2014) used the metaphor of living on the borderlands as an Asian/Japanese transnational cisgendered gay man living in the "thick intersectionalities" (p. 979). Tienari (2019) also wrote about his realization of just how far his privilege could take him as a native Finnish speaker in the world of business and academia in Finland, and how quickly that privilege can be turned upside down after a move to Sweden, where his native tongue no longer afforded the privilege. Such explorations of intersectional identities in IAE often prompt autoethnographers to reconsider or recraft their identities and relationships with others based on their self-discoveries.

Autoethnographers employ intersectional analysis to examine how gender, race, class, religion, ability, sexuality, nationality and other identities are experienced by themselves, and by others, in multiple settings (Alexander, 2016; Bilgen, 2018; Boylorn & Orbe, 2020; Garcia-Fernandez, 2020). Gençoğlu (2020) interrogated the multiple, overlapping, and conflicting identity ambiguities she experienced as a Turkish citizen, a feminist woman, and a political scientist living and working in Turkey during the political upheaval of an attempted coup. She was motivated by a belief that one must understand who one is in the world in order to change what is wrong in the world. To do this, she plunges into the depths of her "emotions and thoughts" in order to understand the "contradictions in the way that [she] perceive[s] the world" (Gençoğlu, 2020, p. 601). She chose autoethnography to help her see herself more clearly, to let go of limiting "fictive distance" between what she most values and how she is able to live, and to see "transformation in the way that politics is conceptualized" (p. 602). Like so many other autoethnographers, a transformative intention was made plain. She desired to create "an implicit solidarity with readers . . . to contribute to an oppositional consciousness and cooperative politics" (p. 603).

Identities are subject to continual deconstructing and reconstructing, becoming undone and redone. The critical self-reflexive processes of IAE are able to pivot one's gaze between individual experience and the power-filled structures in one's culture which shape identity. Autoethnographic grappling with the consequences of belonging to multiple identity categories uncovers the intricacies of power, privilege, and oppression as individual autoethnographers process their experiences, make new identity articulations, and live differently in the negotiated spaces. Individual stories are transported from the "personal to the communal" (Keating & González-López, 2011, p. 2) through both the autoethnographic crafting and telling. As autoethnographers work to integrate their multiple identities, they experience personal change that impacts the quality of their relational experiences, which in turn has the potential for far-reaching transformation beyond the lives of those with whom they interact. Readers are also offered an opportunity for parallel transformative experiences with the authors as they enter the authors' journey, deciding for themselves what meaning to make and apply in their lives.

Emancipating and Decolonizing

The transformative power unleashed through autobiographical and autoethnographic narrative enables autoethnographers to use their own story, told in their own way, as a means of challenging unjust systems and to ignite liberatory responses. Voices that were once silenced as storytellers by colonialism, marginalization, and economic injustice can question, "How does our writing . . . reproduce a system of domination and how does it challenge that system?" (Richardson, 1997, p. 57). In response to this question, autoethnographers can critically interrogate their own "personal and cultural realities" with an eye toward social and cultural change (Boylorn & Orbe, 2020, p. 13). Their stories bring societal issues that have been hidden from view into a public space, transforming what was unseen and silenced into what can be seen and heard. In this new space, new opportunities are imagined to change future storylines, for individuals and the societies they inhabit.

There are some notable individuals who have attempted to do just that. For example, Gloria Anzaldua, a Chicana scholar of cultural theory, feminist theory, and queer theory, wrote openly about her lifelong experiences of social and cultural marginalization at the intersection of her various identities in what she calls the *Borderlands* (1987). Although her work was not clearly identified as autoethnographic, she famously made use of a mixed genre of narrative, autobiographical, testimonial writing that poetically gave voice to fiery activist intention. Her work was instrumental in demonstrating that writing as resistance could accomplish much in the way of mobilizing voices from the margins toward solidarity with the oppressed. Other indigenous scholars have since undertaken autoethnography, using indigenous literary form and style, to bring liberation to the storying process (Chandrashekar, 2018). It is not surprising, therefore that Dutta (2018), in the introduction to a special issue of *Cultural Studies* ↔ *Critical Methodologies*, called auto-ethnography "a radical form" that can unsettle the "colonial violence that is deeply ingrained in the everyday structures" (p. 95).

The privileging of previously silenced voices through autoethnography also enables more emancipatory counter-narratives to emerge. These counter-stories or counter-narratives "expose, analyze, and critique the racialized reality in which those experiences are contextualized, silenced, and perpetuated" (Miller et al., 2020, p. 273). As Ferguson (2017) observed, the "specificity of native histories" (p. 273), spoken in native voices, can counter the narratives that have been interpreted through hegemonic lenses for many years. She argued that these insider voices are needed to get deep and more true, balanced understandings. After all, she argued, "trying to understand colonialism without the voices and histories of indigenous people" is "akin to trying to understand patriarchy without the voices and histories of women" (p. 273). Autoethnography offers a way for the voices to be heard, perhaps explaining why autoethnography is increasingly thought of as the methodology of the oppressed (Diversi & Moreira, 2018). Making space for those previously silenced to speak, to use their position as storyteller, and to reach their own conclusions about themselves as marginalized voices in a colonized world, is itself a transformation of what was previously allowed in academic writing (Bishop, 2020; Chandrashekar, 2018).

Examples are plentiful of autoethnographic narratives that purposefully critique systems of power, making visible and challenging dominant discourses. One example is Hannon's (2017) autoethnographic account that proposed a clear path toward acknowledging the many ways that as a Black man, "we are named by others" and then shows a way to "name ourselves" (p. 167). Likewise Zapata-Sepúlveda (2016) used poetry and prose to uncover her reality as a Latin American living in a world where words like POLITICS, RACISM, SEXISM, and VIOLENCE (left in caps as it appears in her text) have a distinct meaning for an immigrant, outsider, raised inside war zones, where her voice was often censored or restricted. She described autoethnography as freeing—allowing her space "to develop a voice that I had not heard before" (p. 472). Using her own uncovered voice, she was able to "break through the silence that maintains social injustice" (p. 472), thus confronting and challenging the systems of oppression in her life.

These examples suggest transformative exchanges are possible through stories of shared pain around injustices in society when these stories, as well as possible solutions, are told by the ones in pain. As others read and experience these counter narratives, their own story shifts, upsetting the hegemonic narratives within the systems of power in question. In these cases, autoethnography becomes a tool capable of undoing imperialist "Western/White/Eurocentric knowledge claims" and bringing these claims "under the scrutiny of reflexivity," inspiring a "renewed politics of decolonization" (Dutta, 2018, p. 96). Autoethnographers raise their own conscious awareness while empowering their readers to bear witness to and challenge systems of oppression (Okello, 2019). Thus the voices of autoethnographers *speak truth to power* and can sometimes "shame those in power to do the right thing" (Faulkner, 2019, p. 555).

Indigenous people around the globe have long recognized the emancipatory power of story. As stories give their lives coherence and purpose, shape identity, and enhance culture, they also create possibility for change (Soldier, 2017). Through indigenous voices, autoethnography brings "indigenous life worlds and their relation to colonized worlds" into the spotlight, challenging the existing norms of *"Who can speak"* and *"What can be said"* (Henderson, 2019, p. 274).

Constructing one's identity out of "complex webs of oppressive and hegemonic systems" is a defining feature of autoethnography, as a "de/postcolonizing" practice (Toyosaki, 2018, p. 33). Toyosaki, a Japanese scholar navigating colonized academic spaces, lamented the compulsory use of English as only one colonizing feature that often works to silence indigenous and marginalized voices. In his autoethnographic account, he wrote how his "heart feels displaced in doing autoethnography in English" as he, like other nonnative English speakers, may be prone to "reproduce" existing knowledge (p. 35).

By making this tension clear through his autoethnographic writing, Toyosaki departed from knowledge reproduction and instead offered, perhaps surprising even himself, a compelling counter-narrative in his own voice.

Researchers find a way to "push back with indigenous autoethnography" (Bishop, 2020, p. 2) as they describe, resist, and confront oppressive normative practices and use their own storying methods and stylistic manner to tell their own stories. As Bishop (2020) wrote her story as a "Gamilaroi woman belonging to the country now known as Australia," she made it obvious how important it was for her to find a research voice that would be uniquely her own, calling her autoethnography *Don't Tell Me What to Do*. Autoethnographies such as hers illustrate the power of telling one's story in one's own manner as an element that adds to the transformative impact of autoethnography. It is as one uses their individual voice that their single reality is best transfused to others. It is in this shared space that the work of societal transformation can be multiplied.

Summary

In this chapter we have attempted to connect the features of transformative learning as a metatheory with the processes inherent to individual autoethnography. We have highlighted aspects of autoethnography that are necessary for these transformative processes. These are: the power of a single story, the dialogical relationship between the author and the reader/audience, and the autoethnographic intent to discover truth and deepen understanding of social phenomenon toward a transformative goal. As evident from the autoethnographic works reviewed, individual autoethnography can be a powerful tool that is therapeutically healing, useful in shaping identities and relationships, and well suited to challenge systems of oppression and injustice in society. This discussion and the examples referenced lay the groundwork for what is possible as individuals engage in the transformative work of autoethnography.

Autoethnography, done individually, grows outwardly. As it is practiced and shared in the community of others, the individual story is a conduit for deep personal change and connection with others that is transformative. These stories have tremendous potential to impact our lives in positive ways. Writer Joan Didion famously suggested by her book title, *We Tell Ourselves*

Stories in Order to Live. As autoethnographers, we tell our stories autoethnographically in order to live better lives, individually and collectively.

References

Adams, T. E. (2012). *Narrating the closet: An autoethnography of same-sex attraction*. Left Coast Press.

Adams, T. E. (2021). Post–coming out complications. In R. Boylorn and M. Orbe (Eds.), *Critical autoethnography* (pp. 91–102). Routledge.

Alexander, B. K. (2016). Critical autoethnography as intersectional praxis: A performative pedagogical interplay on bleeding borders of identity. In R. Boylorn and M. Orbe (Eds.), *Critical Autoethnography* (pp. 110–122). Routledge.

Anderson, L. & Glass-Coffin, B. (2013). I learn by going. In S. Holman Jones, T. Adams, & C. Ellis (Eds.), *Handbook of autoethnography* (pp. 57–83). Left Coast Press.

Anzaldua, G. (1987). *Borderlands/La Frontera: The new Metiza*. Aunt Lute.

Berry, K. & Patti, C.J. (2015) Lost in narration: Applying autoethnography. *Journal of Applied Communication Research, 43*(2), 263–268. https://doi.org/10.1080/00909882.2015.1019548

Bilgen, W. A. (2018). *Constructing a social justice leadership identity: An autoethnography of a female Jewish Christian social worker living in Turkey*. [Unpublished doctoral dissertation]. Eastern University.

Bishop, M. (2020). "Don't tell me what to do": Encountering colonialism in the academy and pushing back with Indigenous autoethnography. *International Journal of Qualitative Studies in Education, 34*(5), 367–378. https://doi.org/10.1080/09518398.2020.1761475.

Boylorn, R. M., & Orbe, M. P. (Eds.). (2020). *Critical autoethnography: Intersecting cultural identities in everyday life*. Routledge.

Brown, B. (2012, March). *Listening to shame* [Video]. TED Conferences. https://www.ted.com/talks/brene_brown_listening_to_shame

Bruner, J. (1985). Narrative and paradigmatic modes of thought. In E. Eisner (Ed.), *Learning and Teaching the Ways of Knowing*, (pp. 97–115). University of Chicago Press.

Bruner, J. (2004). Life as narrative. *Social Research, 7*(3), 691–710.

Chandrashekar, S. (2018). Not a metaphor: Immigrant of color autoethnography as a decolonial move. *Cultural Studies ↔ Critical Methodologies, 18*(1), 72–79. https://doi.org/10.1177/1532708617728953.

Chang, H., & Bilgen, W. (2020). Autoethnography in leadership studies: Past, present, and future. *Journal of Autoethnography, 1*(1), 93–98. https://doi.org/10.1525/joae.2020.1.1.93

Colyar, J. (2015). Reflections on writing and autoethnography. In S. Holman-Jones, T. E. Adams, & C. Ellis (Eds.), *Handbook of autoethnography* (pp. 263–283). Left Coast.

Conquergood, D. (2002). Performance studies: Interventions and radical research. *The Drama Review, 46*(2), 145–156. https://doi.org/10.1162/105420402320980550.

Culkin, D. T. (2019). A need to continue healing: Report of findings from an autoethnographic study. *The Qualitative Report, 24*(12), 3150–3191. Retrieved from https://nsuworks.nova.edu/tqr/vol24/iss12/14.

Denzin, N. K. (2003). *Performance ethnography: Critical pedagogy and the politics of culture.* SAGE.

Denzin, N. K. (2014). *Interpretive autoethnography.* SAGE.

Denzin, N. K. (2018). *Performance autoethnography: Critical pedagogy and the politics of culture.* Routledge.

Didion, J. (2006). *We tell ourselves stories in order to live: Collected nonfiction* (No. 304). Everyman's Library.

Diversi, M., & Moreira, C. (2018). *Betweener autoethnographies: A path towards social justice.* Routledge.

Dutta, M. J. (2018). Autoethnography as decolonization, decolonizing autoethnography: Resisting to build our homes. *Cultural Studies ↔ Critical Methodologies, 18*(1), 94–96. https://doi.org/10.1177/1532708617735637

Eguchi, S. (2014). Disidentifications from the West(ern): An autoethnography of becoming an Other. *Cultural Studies ↔ Critical Methodologies, 14*(3), 279–285. https://doi.org/10.1177/1532708614527562

Ellis, C. (2004). *The ethnographic I:. Methodological novel about autoethnography.* AltaMira Press.

Ellis, C. (1995). *Final Negotiations: A Story of Love, Loss, and Chronic Illness.* Philadelphia: Temple University Press.

Ellis, C. (2018). *Final negotiations : A story of love, loss, and chronic illness.* ProQuest Ebook Central.

Ellis, C. & Bochner, A. (2017). Forward. In S. Pensoneau-Conway, T. Adams, & D. Bolen (Eds.), *Doing autoethnography* (pp. i–ix). Brill Sense.

Faulkner, S. L. (2019). Shaming as a form of social activism: Autoethnographic stories. *Qualitative Inquiry, 25*(6), 555–558. https://doi.org/10.1177/1077800418806608

Ferdinand, R. (2018). It's like a Black woman's Charlie Brown moment: An autoethnography of being diagnosed with lupus. *Journal of Health Psychology, 23*(12), 1566–1578. https://doi.org/10.1177/1359105316664128

Ferguson, K. E. (2017). Feminist theory today. *Annual Review of Political Science, 20*, 269–286. https://doi.org/10.1146/annurev-polisci-052715-111648

Frank, A. W. (2013). *The wounded storyteller: Body, illness, and ethics.* University of Chicago Press.

García-Fernández, C. (2020). Intersectionality and autoethnography: DeafBlind, DeafDisabled, deaf and hard of hearing-Latinx children are the future. *JCSCORE, 6*(1), 40–67.

Gençoğlu, F. (2020). On the construction of identities: An autoethnography from Turkey. *International Political Science Review, 41*(4), 600–612. https://doi.org/10.1177/0192512119858369

Gerena, C. E. (2019). Conflict between religious beliefs and sexuality: An autoethnography. *The Qualitative Report, 24*(9), 2297-2308. Retrieved from https://nsuworks.nova.edu/tqr/vol24/iss9/14

Gildea, I. J. (2021). The poetry of forgiveness: Poetic inquiry, forgiveness, and autoethnography in the context of childhood sexual abuse (CSA) recovery. *Journal of Spirituality in Mental Health, 23*(1), 77–97.https://doi.org/10.1080/19349637.2020.1729290

Grant, A. (2010). Writing the reflexive self: An autoethnography of alcoholism and the impact of psychotherapy culture. *Journal of Psychiatric and Mental Health Nursing, 17*(7), 577–582. https://doi.org/10.1111/j.1365-2850.2010.01566.x

Hannon, M. D. (2017). Acknowledging intersectionality: An autoethnography of a Black school counselor educator and father of a student with autism. *The Journal of Negro Education, 86*(2), 154–162. https://doi.org/10.7709/jnegroeducation.86.2.0154

Henderson, E. (2019). Researching practitioner experiences through autoethnography: Embodying social policy, exploring emotional landscapes. *Journal of Early Childhood Research, 17*(1), 32–43.https://doi.org/10.1177/1476718X18809135

Herrmann, A. F. (2016). The ghostwriter writes no more: Narrative logotherapy and the mystery of my namesake. *Qualitative Inquiry, 22*(7), 588–599. https://doi.org/10.1177/1077800415622504

Holman Jones, S.., Adams, T., & Ellis, C. (2016). Introduction: Coming to know autoethnography as more than a method. In S. Holman Jones, T. Adams, & C. Ellis (Eds.), *Handbook of Autoethnography* (pp. 17–47). Left Coast Press.

Javaid, A. (2020). Reconciling an irreconcilable past: Sexuality, autoethnography, and reflecting on the stigmatization of the "unspoken." *Sexualities, 23*(7), 1199–1227. https://doi.org/10.1177/1363460719888434

Keating, A., & Gonzalez-Lopez, G. (Eds.). (2011). *Bridging: How Gloria Anzaldúa's life and work transformed our own.* Austin: University of Texas Press.

Kirsch, A. (2020, May 4). Søren Kierkegaard's struggle with himself. *The New Yorker.* https://www.newyorker.com/magazine/2020/05/11/soren-kierkegaards-struggle-with-himself

Leavy, P. (2020). *Method meets art: Arts-based research practice.* Guilford Publications.

Lengelle, R. (2016). Narrative self-rescue: A poetic response to a precarious labour crisis. *New Horizons in Adult Education and Human Resource Development, 28*(1), 46–49. https://doi.org/10.1002/nha3.20130

Lengelle, R. (2021). *Writing the self in bereavement: A story of love, spousal loss, and resilience.* Routledge.

Matthews, A. (2019). Writing through grief: Using autoethnography to help process grief after the death of a loved one. *Methodological Innovations, 12*(3). https://doi.org/10.1177/2059799119889569

McIlveen, P. (2008). Autoethnography as a method for reflexive research and practice in vocational psychology. *Australian Journal of Career Development, 17*(2), 13–20. https://doi.org/10.1177/103841620801700204

Melrose, S. (2010). Naturalistic generalization. In A. Mills, G. Durepos, & E. Wiebe (Eds.), *Encyclopedia of Case Study Research* (pp. 600–601). SAGE.

Metta, M. (2013). Putting the body on the line. In S. Holman Jones, T. Adams, & C. Ellis (Eds.), *Handbook of autoethnography* (pp. 486–510). Left Coast Press.

Mezirow, J., & Associates (1990). *Fostering critical reflection in adulthood: A guide to transformative and emancipatory learning.* Jossey-Bass.

Micklethwaite, D., & Earle, R. (2021). A voice within: An autoethnographic account of moving from closed to open prison conditions by a life-sentenced prisoner. *The Howard Journal of Crime and Justice.* https://doi.org/10.1111/hojo.12430

Miller, R., Liu, K., & Ball, A. F. (2020). Critical counter-narrative as transformative methodology for educational equity. *Review of Research in Education, 44*(1), 269–300. https://doi.org/10.3102/0091732X20908501

Moffitt, K. R. (2020). "Light-skinned people always win": An autoethnography of colorism in a mother–daughter relationship. *Women, Gender, and Families of Color, 8*(1), 65–86. https://doi.org/10.5406/womgenfamcol.8.1.0065

Okello, W. (2019). "I wanted the world to see": Black feminist performance auto/ethnography. In N.K. Denzin & M.D. Giardina (Eds.), *Qualitative Inquiry at a Crossroads* (pp. 32–47). Routledge.

O'Shea, S. C. (2019). My dysphoria blues: Or why I cannot write an autoethnography. *Management Learning, 50*(1), 38–49. https://doi.org/10.1177/1350507618791115

Pelias, R. J. (1999). *Writing performance: Poeticizing the researcher's body.* SIU Press.

Pelias, R. J. (2010). Performance is an opening. *International Review of Qualitative Research, 3*(2), 173–174. https://doi.org/10.1525/irqr.2010.3.2.173

Reed-Danahay, D. (Ed.). (2021). *Auto/ethnography: Rewriting the self and the social.* Routledge. (Original work published 1997)

Richards, R. (2008). Writing the othered self: Autoethnography and the problem of objectification in writing about illness and disability. *Qualitative Health Research, 18*(12), 1717–1728. https://doi.org/10.1177/1049732308325866

Richards, R. (2019) Shame, silence and resistance: How my narratives of academia and kidney disease entwine. *Feminism & Psychology, 29*(2), 269–285. https://doi.org/10.1177/09593535 18786757

Richardson, L. (1997). *Fields of play: Constructing an academic life.* Rutgers University Press.

Ross, S. L. (2020). A concept analysis of the form that trans-forms as a result of transformation. *International Journal of Psychological Studies, 12*(2), 52. https://doi.org//10.5539/ijps.v12n2p52

Schapiro, S. A., Gallegos, P. V., Stashower, K., & Clark, D. F. (2017). Reflections on the 12th international transformative learning conference: Engaging at the intersections of theory and practice. *Journal of Transformative Education, 15*(1), 6–15. https://doi.org/10.1177/1541344616685644

Short, N. P., Turner, L., & Grant, A. (2013). *Contemporary British autoethnography.* Rotterdam, Netherlands: SensePublishers.

Soldier, L. L. (2017). *Whereas: Poems.* Graywolf Press.

Sparkes, A. C. (2018). Autoethnography comes of age: Consequences, comforts, and concerns. In D. Beach, C. Bagley, and S. Da Silva (Eds.) *The Wiley handbook of ethnography of education* (pp. 479–499). John Wiley & Sons.

Speedy, J. (2013). Where the wild dreams are fragments from the spaces between research, writing, autoethnography, and psychotherapy. *Qualitative Inquiry, 19*(1), 27–34. https://doi.org/10.1177/1077800412462980

Spry, T. (2011) Performative autoethnography: Critical embodiments and possibilities. In N. K. Denzin, & Y. S. Lincoln (Eds.) *The SAGE Handbook of Qualitative Research* (pp. 497–511). SAGE.

Stahlke Wall, S. (2016). Toward a moderate autoethnography. *International Journal of Qualitative Methods.* https://doi.org/10.1177/1609406916674966

Tienari, J. (2019). One flew over the duck pond: Autoethnography, academic identity, and language. *Management Learning, 50*(5), 576–590. https://doi.org/10.1177/1350507619875887

Tisdell, E. J. (2012). Themes and variations of transformational learning: Interdisciplinary perspectives on forms that transform. In E. W. Taylor, & P. Cranton (Eds.), *The Handbook of Transformative Learning: Theory, Research, and Practice*, (pp. 21–36). San Francisco: Jossey-Bass.

Tisdell, E. J. (2017). Transformative pilgrimage learning and spirituality on the Caminio de Santiago. In *Transformative Learning Meets Bildung* (pp. 341–352). Brill Sense.

Toyosaki, S. (2018). Toward de/postcolonial autoethnography: Critical relationality with the academic second persona. *Cultural Studies ↔ Critical Methodologies 18*(1), 32–42. https://doi.org/10.1177/1532708617735133

Villanueva, G. (2020). Making place for my space/making space for our displacement: An embodied autoethnography of a reflexive communicative urban planner. *Cultural Studies ↔ Critical Methodologies, 20*(2), 157–166. https://doi.org/10.1177/1532708619879197

White, M., & Epston, D. (1990). *Narrative Means to Therapeutic Ends*. W.W. Norton.

Witkin, S. L. (Ed.). (2014). *Narrating social work through autoethnography*. Columbia University Press.

Wyatt, J. (2021). Frank and the gift, or the untold told: Provocations for autoethnography and therapy. In T. Adams, S. Holman Jones, & C. Ellis (Eds.) *Handbook of Autoethnography* (pp. 79–88). Routledge.

Zapata-Sepúlveda, P. (2016). One continent, three words, and a dream: Making interpretive [auto]ethnography in a particular place in northern Chile. *Qualitative Inquiry, 22*(6), 472–475. https://doi.org/10.1177/1077800415617203

THREE

Collaborative Autoethnography (CAE) for Transformation

Kathy-Ann's Story

WHEN I, ALONG WITH TWO other colleagues, began a collaborative autoethnography exploring our experiences as foreign-born women of color in the United States' predominantly White academy, we were not fully prepared for where this journey would take us. Yes, we had each been involved in individual autoethnographic work and even collaborative work, but we soon realized that this was different. In the process of unearthing stories of the challenges we faced in making our way in the academy, something profound was happening in each of us. We were changing individually and collectively. I suppose I could have expected this given the personal nature of autoethnographic work, but cognitive knowledge is very different from experiential knowledge.

Something unique happened when we held up our personal experience for each other to examine. We were baring much of our hidden selves and prodding and provoking each other to look closer at those experiences—to corner and wring the last bit of meaning out of them. It was awkward, even uncomfortable, and our dialogical exchanges were sometimes confrontational. However, in the process of engaging in this kind of deep work, we were able to discover ourselves and others with a kind of microscopic focus that had not been present in our previous work. As we reflected on and wrote about our individual experiences in coming to this point in our journey, we discovered commonalities and differences. The most unexpected gift was that we discovered new ways of thinking about our experiences that empowered us to view our challenges not from points of marginalization but as unique positionalities. We were emboldened to flex our scholarly muscles and to turn a perceived threat into a point of strength, to *exploit the margins* (Hernandez et al., 2014). Through the communal process of exploring how we navigated higher education at the intersection of our various identities, we found hope and courage to continue.

****

Autoethnographers often choose to work in groups to investigate issues of mutual interest. This approach to autoethnographic work continues to evolve to benefit scholarship and practice. As has been discussed in the previous chapters, the appearance of autoethnographic inquiry has given researchers space to position themselves squarely in the social science research field, which had in some respects siloed researchers' voices as merely tools in the research process. The multidisciplinary applications of individual and collaborative approaches also provide ample evidence that the experiences of researchers can contribute significantly to our understanding of social phenomena, and at the same time yield transformative results for those involved. The growing body of literature, as well as our own experiences, convinces us that "collaborative autoethnography can be an important tool whereby scholars can create community, advance scholarship, and be empowered to effect changes at their institution even as they negotiate their own advancement" (Hernandez et al., 2014, p. 16). In this chapter, we review collaborative autoethnography, highlight its transformative capacity, and elaborate on how it is operationalized at the personal, communal, and organizational level.

CAE Methodology

A variety of terms have been used to describe autoethnographic work done in community, such as duo-autoethnography (Sawyer & Norris, 2013), community autoethnography (Toyosaki et al., 2009), or co/autoethnography (McPhail-Bell & Redman-MacLaren, 2019; Taylor & Coia, 2020). Chang et al. (2013) labeled it collaborative autoethnography (CAE) and defined it as "a qualitative research method in which researchers work in community to collect their autobiographical materials and to analyze and interpret these data collectively to gain a meaningful understanding of sociocultural phenomena reflective in their autobiographical data" (p. 24). This label has been adopted by a multitude of community-oriented autoethnographers (Carless & Douglas, 2022; Lapadat, 2017).

Irrespective of how it is labeled, CAE involves the investigation of social phenomena in the company of one or more other researchers. It embodies all four critical dimensions of autoethnographic work. First, it is self-focused, involving the interrogation of self using autobiographical data. Second, it is context-conscious, so that data are understood in the context of the inter-action between researcher participants and the ecological spaces they have inhabited. Third, it is researcher-visible, in that the thoughts, experiences, and perspective of the researcher are visible in a dynamic reflexive process as the researcher moves back and forth from the roles of researchers and participant. Fourth, it is critically dialogic because researchers are engaged in a critical internal dialogue moving between the dual roles of researcher and participant as well as further dialogue with the other coautoethnogra-phers who are part of the CAE team (see Chang et al., 2013). CAE offers the deep-level internal processing of individual autoethnography with the added benefit of undergoing such explorations with others who are also intent on understanding a selected phenomenon.

CAE researchers benefit from a variety of approaches to collecting and analyzing the data while working in community. Unlike individual autoeth-nography, in which one researcher is the participant, a collaborative auto-ethnography project includes others, and it is not bound by a singular de-mographic or geographic boundary. Individuals from different racial/ethnic backgrounds, other socioidentity markers, and/or geographic or spatial loca-tions can choose to collaborate. CAE involves a symphony of voices and per-spectives working in community. Such explorations span the spectrum, rang-ing from more analytical approaches to highly evocative approaches (Ngunjiri et al., 2010), and often mirror the disciplinary foci of the CAE research team. Data collection can take place concurrently, with all the data collected from participants in real time such as in a focus group discussion, or sequentially, as in the form of a threaded discussion board where the ideas and insights of one participant trigger the ideas and thoughts of others. Depending on the particular research slant, evocative or analytical, researchers can meet to consolidate their memory data and to determine in community or with a lead autoethnographer how to present the final CAE project deliverable.

The book *Collaborative Autoethnography* (Chang et al., 2013) provides a detailed discussion of collaborative autoethnography framed through an ana-lytic lens, whereas Ellis and Bochner and Ellis (2016) present a comprehensive account of evocative autoethnography (see also Ellis, 2008). Though the latter were written specifically for individual autoethnography, the same methods and strategies can be applied to work done in community. These resources pro-vide detailed accounts of the theory and how-to of autoethnographic research with a distinct scholarly focus. In keeping with the intent of this book, we focus our discussion on how autoethnography can be used by practitioners.

The Transformative Capacity of CAE

Some researchers have turned the spotlight on the transformative element in autoethnography, highlighting especially how autoethnography has been a tool for transformative learning (see, for example, Boyd, 2008; Custer, 2014; Sykes, 2014). However, many of these works have been more descriptive than prescriptive. More often than not, as was noted in the CAE project described in the opening section, the transformative aspect of AE has often been a by-product of such work. This was the case in a nine-month-long investigation of how immersion in sponsorship relationships shaped the way individuals developed their leadership identities. One unexpected finding from that project was that the communal process of engaging in the CAE project over that extended period of time proved to have a transforming effect on how these participants' came to think of themselves as leaders (Hernandez & Longman, 2020). Likewise, Longman et al. (2015) found that in their study designed to uncover the mentorship experiences of leaders within their institutional context, the CAE process in and of itself created a space for the formation of mentorship relationships and transformation in their leadership identity. As the authors noted, "The positive experiences during the CAE project contributed to the participants developing a more realistic and uplifting image of themselves" (p. 218).

In spite of this transformative element of the autoethnographic process, little has been written specifically focusing on that. Apart from the research process itself, the process of engaging in AE/CAE is inherently transformative. It is this transformative capacity that can have many positive applications for practitioners and scholars who seek to use the method to move beyond informing practice to changing it. We focus here, therefore, on selected features of collaborative autoethnography that have applicability for work with a primarily transformative intent.

Multivocality and the Discovery of Self and Others

Collaborative autoethnography (CAE) is distinguished from individual autoethnography (IAE) by the practical and philosophical implications that attend the integration of multiple researchers/participants to the investigation of a central phenomenon. This multivocal element operates differently in CAE as compared to IAE. Though multivocality is present in individual work where the researcher can be positioned as embarking on an interrogation of experiences with their various selves and in relation to others, collaborative work complicates such interrogations in important ways. The complexity of CAE interrogations overlays the interrogation of various selves at the individual level, within the outer layer of the group context. Thus multivocality is compounded exponentially as individual interrogations become part of the larger community of voices relevant to the topic.

Collaborative autoethnography is particularly useful in bridging differences. In some CAE projects, individuals have worked across disparities to facilitate a deeper understanding of the unique space that others occupy. This willingness to embark on a journey to understand the world from another perspective invites participants to build community across cultural divides and can provide insights that facilitate mutual understanding. Nevertheless, there are not enough instances in the literature where CAE has been used for the specific purpose of troubling those differences to create a shared understanding of others and their varied perspectives.

Cross-racial autoethnographies often provide a space for individuals of different racial/ethnic groups to address contentious differences with a view to facilitating knowledge shifts and understanding. Lund and Nabavi (2008) embarked on a brave examination of their different frames of reference as a White male and female of color respectively. Through exploring their unique perspectives at the intersection of their various identities of race and gender, they were able to create a microcommunity of difference nevertheless united in their collective exploration of activism among young people. Similarly, Shametrice Davis, a woman of color, and Chris Linder, a White woman, used CAE to talk through their distinct perspectives as individuals committed to an antiracist research and activism agenda (Davis & Linder, 2017). Their work offered a transparent account of the complexity and challenges of such discourse where sometimes the final outcome is simply to agree to disagree. At the same time, in the process of choosing to engage dialogically, and despite the struggle of doing so across profound differences, neither of them could leave such an encounter unchanged. Though such CAE explorations may not be able to bridge the differences gap completely, they do offer a space to center the voices of many.

To be able to discover others, we must embark on the challenging task of finding a way to privilege all voices in the discourse. As we have seen, the mul-tivocal quality that CAE possesses allows for the creation of a space that can foster community across differences. However, multivocality presents both opportunities and challenges, especially in CAE projects involving many par-ticipants. Each participant's perspective is viewed as part of the community dialogic process and search for meaning-making. Even though the voices may not make it into the final published piece or product, the process of dialoguing about the data can change the community in unanticipated ways. The mutual sharing and meaning making cannot be undone; it changes the individuals within the space and shapes the process, if not the final product.

However, it is a challenge to present all voices well. Choosing to make the data collection, interpretation, and reporting process transparent is a useful strategy in honoring this strength of CAE work (Anfara et al., 2002; Denzin & Lincoln, 2005). For example, in writing a piece on "mothering" with seven other participants, Geist-Martin et al. (2010) found that sharing their moth-ering experiences both challenged and united members of the seven-person CAE team in unanticipated ways. In their published article, the authors shared their lived experiences of mothering, discussed the issues surrounding them, critiqued their own assumptions as they arose, and then collaborated to edit and parse their stories and findings into a digestible format. However, they struggled with how best to capture what they found from their explorations, and admitted this in the final published piece:

> We felt the "cut" of shortening these stories quite deeply; every time we shortened the narratives, our (once rich and descriptive) autoethnographic narratives felt more shallow . . . and of course the question also emerged on a seven-person author team of "who decides what to cut?" (p. 4)

Similarly, in recounting the backstory to a CAE project that was eventually published, Hernandez (Bieri et al., 2022) discussed the challenge she faced in having to advocate strongly with the journal editors to keep the multivo-cal element of their work instead of only writing up results where there was majority consensus. Those voices and differing perspectives were part of the work. The multiplicative effect of interrogations in such a research project provides opportunities for both individual and group transformation, and those voices and experiences are a salient part of the research finding.

This positionality is critical since, as a qualitative method, collaborative autoethnography at once adheres to *and* challenges traditional approaches of data analysis and interpretation. The method is built on extracting perspectives of the collective (collaborative) but not privileging it at the expense of the individual (auto). Thus CAE work advocates an intentional representation of multiple voices of participants that may not conform neatly to a common theme/idea. In this way, it gives voice to the range of individual perspectives—multivocality. That is a strength of CAE. The multivocal challenge in many ways also presents a useful check on the disciplinary and research bias that reduces data to the most frequent or prevalent observations. It turns the spotlight on the dialogical process in CAE that is inherent in the transformative outcome of such work.

CAE Community Building, Solidarity, and Support

Inherent in the collaborative autoethnography process is interaction among research participants. One of the distinct advantages of CAE from other kinds of research collaborations is the level of intimacy that it can engender through sharing of personal data. Not surprisingly, community-building has often emerged as a distinctive feature of such collaborative work. CAE is able to do this as it offers unique opportunities for groups to develop solidarity and discovery of self in community with others (Chang et al., 2013; Hernandez & Longman, 2020). Blalock and Akehi (2018), for example, discovered that the CAE practice of intentionally creating space to share their experiences frankly "drew us closer together in friendship and scholarship" (p. 91). A group of four African American women who used CAE to reflect on a "doctoral sister circle" cited authentic community as one of three major supports that the circle offered them (Teasdell et al., 2021). And Whalen and Simmons (2021) described the bond that formed through their collaborative exploration of maternal grief where they "provided each other the strength to be vulnerable" (p. 11).

In the case of minorities and/or people of color, the context of sharing in the exploration of a common social issue provides a space for individuals to find support for navigating challenging life issues. The ability to hear some of their own struggles and concerns reflected in the voices of other participants can be liberating and useful in uniting individuals around a common struggle.

To illustrate further, in the previously referenced study on the role of sponsorship in the leadership development of people of color situated in predominantly White spaces, participants highlighted the value of communal sharing and support as an important contributor to their leadership identity development. Over the course of the study, collaborative autoethnography emerged as "a very potent relational dynamic of support" for leadership development as the targeted practice of sponsorship itself (Hernandez & Longman, 2020, p. 134; see also Chang et al., 2014). This finding is consistent with what others found with respect to CAE research in the context of the academy (Hargons et al., 2017; Johnson et al., 2020; Pak et al., 2021). To this end, CAE has been recommended as a potentially useful tool for fostering community building for people of color and women, particularly in the context of White, male-dominated academic spaces (Hernandez & Longman, 2020).

As with other kinds of collaborative work, community-building often emerges as an unintended outcome of CAE as researchers develop relational bonds that extend beyond the CAE project. In some instances, as is often the case in the academic "publish or perish" landscape, these bonds provide a ready and practical solution to advancing scholarship as a community of scholars invested in the study of a particular phenomenon. It is as common to see an extended list of publications emanating from a particular CAE team as it is for other forms of research collaborations in various disciplines. This points to the building of community that is inherent in teamwork. For example, we can trace the evolution of a research team through the work of Judith Lapadat and her coresearchers. What initially began as a class project involving collaboration between faculty and graduate students continued five years later to the published piece (Lapadat et. al., 2010). However, whereas CAE shares this common capacity to foster team-building as research teams employing other methods of inquiry, the personal and autobiographical sharing that is inherent in CAE lends itself to a more intimate kind of community.

For collaborative autoethnography projects to be effective in fully extricating the essence of the phenomenon under inquiry, it is often necessary for emotional and psychological walls to be breached. CAE in particular is effective at dismantling power differentials in relationships that might have begun as hierarchical—there is a leveling of the relational field to facilitate the kind of personal sharing that the method requires. Examples of such collaborations abound as in the case of Hernandez and Murray-Johnson's (2015) collaborative work between a professor and a former student to investigate emerging constructions of Blackness as foreign-born Caribbean women now situated in the United States. Or that of Zou et al.'s (2020) collaborative team based in Hong Kong, whose intentional negotiation of identities enabled them to leverage hierarchical power structures rather than experience them as a threat. Outside of academia, grieving mothers have used CAE to challenge the uniformly bleak view of maternal bereavement, discovering in their shared brokenness a strength to learn and be transformed (Whalen & Simmons, 2021). Even in the case of coautoethnographers where there is a lead researcher who may not share the experience under investigation (see Ellis et al., 1997), the process of engaging in CAE can unite participants in an intimate communal bond that is part of the research process.

As coauthors of this book, we have benefitted from this kind of community-building in research teams. Chang, who was the dissertation chair for Wendy Bilgen (2018), has gone on to publish with her and now we are collaborating on this book together. Similarly, Chang, Hernandez, and Ngunjiri (Hernandez et al., 2014; Hernandez et al., 2017) have continued to advance scholarship on collaborative autoethnography as a trio and sometimes duo since we began our collaborative work many years ago. Through continued collaborations, we continue to produce and publish research emanating from CAE even as involvement in those lines of inquiry continues to shape us personally and professionally.

Generative Learning and Negotiated Meaning

Autoethnographic work that is done in the company of others offers a level of critical dialogic engagement that is integral to the transformative process. In community, meanings must be teased out and negotiated with much probing and discussion. In the process of arriving at these negotiated meanings, individuals are constantly being challenged to integrate new information and insights into their existing schema. The idea of generative learning is critical to such interrogations. Generative learning occurs when the individual constructs two kinds of mental relationships: (a) those between concepts; and (b) those between prior learning or experience and new information (Wittrock, 1974; 1989). It involves questioning beliefs and assumptions, combined with the adoption of a profound shift in mindset that ultimately expands the ability to create and innovate (Chiva & Habib, 2015; Senge, 2006).

Engagement with multiple perspectives is a cornerstone in teaching and learning that is aligned with a social constructivist perspective. Social constructivists posit that we acquire knowledge through the process of socially interacting with others and considering opinions and perspectives. This kind of social engagement is the basis for the development of knowledge and socially relevant skills. Confronted with ideas and opinions which may differ from what an individual originally thought, they must adapt and begin the process of creating or constructing new schemas or ways of thinking about a topic or issue. In sum, knowledge construction is a social activity; it comes out of social interaction, is dialogic, and is a shared rather than an individual experience (Prawat & Floden, 1994). Bakhtin (1984) expressed it this way: "Truth is not to be found inside the head of an individual person, it is born between people collectively searching for truth, in the process of their dialogic interaction" (p. 110). Engagement in autoethnographic work that is collaborative is well aligned with the concept of socially constructed learning.

In our work together (Kathy-Ann and Heewon) this search for truth or the "negotiated meaning" aspect of collaborative work has often been, paradoxically, the most contentious and the most beneficial element of our work. This was the case for us in the aforementioned article (Hernandez et al., 2014) on many levels. First, we were challenged to expand our individual perspectives in deciding on a theoretical perspective to ground the work. Would it be informed by psychological leadership or by anthropological theories given our respective disciplinary focuses? Later on, as we met to discuss the meaning for the themes that we saw emerging from the data, we were not always all in agreement that the theme captured us individually. Altogether, when faced with these issues, we sought to make it transparent to the reader by employing multivocal perspectives in our writing. However, the real work was happening within us internally, as the voices that had been raised in our dialogues continued to inform our thinking and in some cases our actions long after the study was completed. These less visible elements of critical dialogue and self-reflection were pivotal to our transformative learning.

As mentioned in Chapter One, Mezirow's theory of transformative learning is an attempt to make visible through a multistep process the workings of this kind of transformative learning. According to Mezirow (2006), *transformative learning* can be defined as the emancipatory process of becoming critically aware of how and why the structure of psychocultural assumptions has come to constrain the way we see ourselves and our relationships, reconstituting this structure to permit a more inclusive and discriminating integration of experience and acting upon these new understandings. (p. 6)

In his earlier work, Mezirow (1978; 1981) focused on the change that happens in the individual through this kind of interaction. However, in his later work, he focused on how transformation at the individual level can have a multiplicative effect as transformed individuals are able to effect changes in both existing and future relationships (Kitchenham, 2008).

Altogether, collaborative autoethnography offers a rich space for critical dialogue which creates a kind of dissonance that can change individual mental models. The critical dialogic element is a potent and often confrontational process through which transformation of knowledge structures can take place. Though sometimes contentious, CAE is at its best when interactions bend towards dialogue rather than debate. In this way, participants can openly engage and reflect on a topic in community to arrive at a deeper understanding of an issue (Sawyer & Norris, 2009). The dialogue is enriched "as autoethnographers work together, building on each other's stories, gaining insights from the group sharing, and providing various levels of support as they interrogate topics of interest" (Chang et al., 2013, p. 23). It is this aspect of collective dialogue and meaning making that "has the potential to break down silos and build theoretical bridges across disciplines and perspectives" (Ngunjiri et al., 2017, pp. 110–111).

CAE and Transformation at Various Levels

We have defined *transformation* in the context of autoethnography as significant changes in cognitive, affective, behavioral, and/or psychological domains that can take place in individuals, communities, and organizations through the process of autoethnographic inquiry. In keeping with this definition, transformation of the self occurs through the critically dialogic process where individuals are positioned to engage in deeper self-reflection through the combined synergies of interactions that take place at the personal level (intrapersonal reflection) and through interactions that are the result of group level processes (interpersonal interactions). Figure 3.1 illustrates the complexity of these interactions between individual autoethnographers and others within their contexts, as well as the compounded interactional effect among the other autoethnographers within a collaborative autoethnography team.

It is through this compounded group effect that individuals and groups are positioned to achieve a deeper and more nuanced transformation. Their engagement in the group process works to transform them, the group, and the wider contexts in which they are situated.

Transformation of the Self in CAE

Transformation in collaborative autoethnography begins at the individual level. Drawing on some of the best features of autoethnographic explorations,

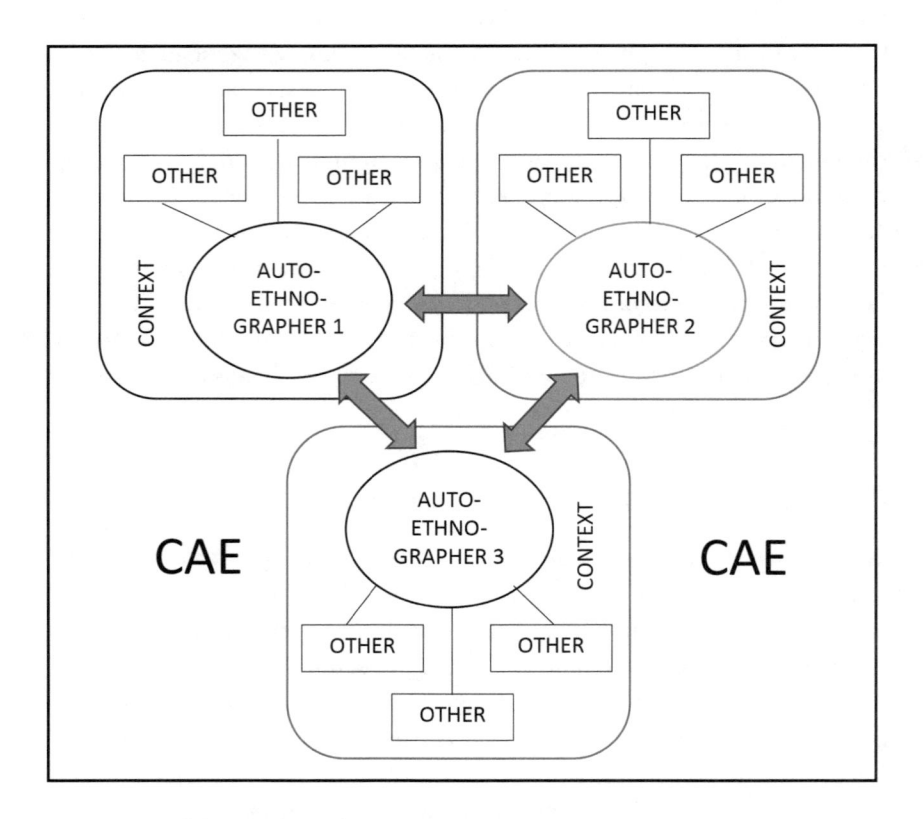

Figure 3.1. Collaborative Autoethnography (CAE)

engaging in self-reflection in the company of others challenges us to step outside of our own heads. We are also invited to embrace different perspectives and frameworks for thinking through our experiences. Collaborative work often challenges inquirers to view their experiences from the multifocal perspective of their combined disciplinary lenses.

For example, in our previous work (Hernandez et al., 2014), we often began with individual writing relevant to question prompts. These pieces of autobiographical data were then shared with CAE team members, who inserted follow-up questions and prompts. These prompts provoked individual autoethnographers to delve deeper into an exploration of their thinking and various selves. Later, these interrogations were discussed in the community for further insight and understanding. In this communal space of follow-up interviews, group discussions, and meaning-making, we have challenged each other with probing questions that provoked the other to reexamine recollections and/or writing—to do so at a microscopic level and to uncover hidden insights about who they are and how they made sense of these experiences—to even critique their thinking about what the experiences mean.

In engaging in this kind of shared meaning, we have also found a common and divergent language to capture our experiences. As noted previously, the critically dialogic process of CAE celebrates multiple voices and perspectives by giving room within the community to hear and represent various voices. This back-and-forth dynamic of voice and representation in the CAE spaces allows researchers space to gain clarity about how their experiences and journeys with particular phenomena are similar to and/or distinct from the other. Hence, coming out of these experiences, the individual researcher gains a level of insight about self and is changed through the processes of gaining the understanding as part of their schema. Sztandara (2021) speaks of the dynamics and complexities of finding this kind of "third space" for negotiating academic and activist identities through the ethnographic process. Nicol and Yee (2017) used the reflexivity of CAE to discover and articulate their insights around navigating academia as women of color, explaining how they arrived at the primacy of self-care in their journey. In this way, the changes that occur in self are inextricably linked to community probing and sharing.

As discussed in the previous chapter, transformation of self is inherent in ethnographic work. At the individual level, we experience change as we reflect on our memory data and probe our thinking and understanding relevant to what happened. In the context of collaborative autoethnography, we are further challenged to invite voices into the space of our interrogations. In the process of engaging in dialogue with others whose experiences may be similar or different from us, we are often challenged to rethink and even question our own recollections. This can lead to deeper interrogations and frames of reference for thinking about our personal experiences. At the same time, based on our disciplinary foci, we might be challenged to think of things differently, applying other theoretical frameworks introduced to us by others in the research team.

Transformation of Others in CAE

Multivocality is inherent in autoethnographic work. However, the critical element that distinguishes CAE from IAE is the practical and philosophical implications that attend the integration of multiple researchers/participants to the investigation of a central phenomenon and the attendant transformative benefits. CAE benefits from the interaction that takes place at the individual level for each autoethnographer as well as the multiplicative interaction effect that takes place among members of the autoethnographic team and the group process.

In individual autoethnographic explorations, we realize as we probe deeper that we are engaging with our various selves in a journey to deeper understanding (Allen-Collinson, 2013; Lapina, 2018; Mizzi, 2010). We can trace the journey of the individual autoethnographer as embarking on an interrogation with their various selves through recollection of personal experiences. A series of dialogical encounters occurs as the autoethnographer engages others in interactive interviewing and other forms of self/other examination with the intention to bring something to light that, without the insight of the another viewpoint, would go unnoticed, unchallenged, unexamined, and unchanged (Denzin, 2003). Harkening back to the notion that our self stories are always performed in the community of others, Denzin (2003) remarked that "the autoethnographer invites members of the community to become co-performers in a drama of social resistance and social critique . . . offering emotional support to one another, coperformers bear witness to the need for social change" (p. 17). In this way, the dialogical process in IAE is bidirectional, having the capacity to evoke changes in both the researcher and the reader/audience.

Individual autoethnographers also interact with others through a review of the literature, as well as by engaging in interactive interviewing of others in their relational network to get a deeper understanding of the topic of their inquiry. These many voices represent important checks for the solo autoethnographer to rethink, reexamine, and probe further their own understanding of recollected events, thus leading the way for new insights and or discoveries (Denzin, 2003).

These various voices and inquiry processes are also present in CAE as the foundational elements of the work. However, they exist in more complex iterations. Firstly, they are present at the individual level for each participant in the CAE project. However, there is the added dimension of voices of the actual participants in the collaborative project as they pool together their various experiences, engage in critical dialogues about these experiences, probe each other about what they mean, and work together to make meaning of it all. Thus, in the context of CAE, multivocality is compounded exponentially as individual examinations become part of the larger community of voices relevant to the topic. The multiplicative effect of these interrogations provides opportunities for transformation at both the individual and group level consistent with the aforementioned understanding of learning as being socially constructed.

This feature of autoethnography is particularly evident in collaborative projects in which autoethnographers occupy positions of differences. It is in these instances that CAE offers unique opportunities for researchers to borrow the lens of the other in a very intimate kind of perspective sharing that has the capacity to change how each participant understands the phenomenon post-CAE project. For example, in their exploration of what it means to be foreign-born Black women in the U.S. academy, Hernandez and Murray-Johnson (2015) recognized that their differing lengths of stay in the United States shaped their emerging constructions of Blackness. At the same time, they were able to gain deeper insight into the perspective of the other. Similarly, Mainsah and his collaborating author Prøitz (2015) relied on their birth differences—one a Cameroonian male, the other a Korean female—to explore how research around race was produced in the Norwegian context. In the CAE process, where they explored other's perspectives, they unearthed their motivations for the research focus that resonated with each as scholars. In another example, Williams, a professor, and Jauhari, a student, chose to analyze Jauhari's earlier experience in the Singaporian Rude Boy culture in a way that would "explore and extend the collaborative nature of autoethnographic accounting in a way that does justice to the multiple voices that create it" (Williams & Jauhari, 2016, p. 37). Each author experienced the process differently: Jauhari found the process freeing, enabling him to reconcile experiences from his youth, while Williams discovered his perspective of scholarship, knowledge-creation, and teaching was broadened. This capacity that CAE affords for an intimate exploration of the perspective of others who may be different from oneself, holds tremendous potential for working across differences to promote understanding and as a tool in conflict resolution efforts.

In general, CAE, like other such qualitative methodologies, offers researchers opportunities to confront different perspectives with microscopic precision. However, CAE is unique in that the intimate level of sharing that takes place in CAE has the potential to tap into a deeper level of empathetic understanding. It can challenge researchers to dialogue through their different viewpoints in the act of perspective taking. Through this process, individual researchers are themselves transformed even as they transform others through the dynamic process of socially constructing meaning in community.

Transformation of Groups in CAE

The group transformation that can take place in CAE is a dynamic function of the interactions at the individual and group level. Namely, as individuals engage in individual and group exploration of self and others in community, these multilayered interactions ultimately change the community. At a very mundane level, the group will undoubtedly change over time as its members function as a collaborative unit to research and sometimes present and/or publish work. In keeping with dynamics of group process first developed by Tuckman (1965), they will experience the steps of "forming," "storming," "norming," "performing," and ultimately "adjourning" (see Tuckman & Jensen, 1977) while working through some of the inherent challenges in group work. In the first two stages of forming and storming, the group becomes oriented to the shared CAE task and tests boundaries, eventually encountering some degree of conflict, resistance, and polarization around issues (Bonebright, 2010). From there, the participants develop cohesion (norming) and then achieve the role flexibility to channel energy into the task at hand (performing). An adjourning stage, where separation of the group occurs upon fulfilment of the project, concludes the CAE enterprise (Tuckman & Jensen, 1977). The very act of working together changes the group and can be harnessed for outcomes of the group's choosing as desired.

In another respect, the group can also change as it interacts with the topic under exploration and the members who are part of that community. The longer the period of collaboration, the greater the opportunities for changes that are substantive and long lasting rather than transitory. In one CAE project which extended over a nine-month period, 17 emerging scholars of color forged a community with each other that extended beyond the research study in question (Hernandez & Longman, 2020). In another example, five researchers explored their relationships—which included friend, sibling, colleague, stranger—and found those relationships altered through the CAE process. Siblings developed a deeper appreciation for the impact of trauma on their relationship. Colleagues and friends found their relationships off the page altered and a community of scholars inspired through the project (Pensoneau-Conway et al., 2014). The research process transformed the group and its members beyond the purpose of the study.

In sum, as participants within the CAE group experience changes within themselves, this also changes the dynamic of the group—there is a layer of change at both the individual and group level that is dynamic and iterative. The change continues as the group members interact with each other and continue to explore social phenomena.

Summary

Since its emergence on the scene many years ago, autoethnographic work continues to challenge our understanding of the nature of research. As discussed in this chapter, it has also inadvertently worked to challenge what constitutes the outcomes or deliverables of research.

Embedded in academic spaces as a unique approach to investigating social phenomena, usage of collaborative autoethnography in the academy has been focused on social inquiry with a view to adding to scholarship on relevant issues. However, there is ample evidence in the literature of its applicability to effecting change in its participants and the contexts in which they exist. The potency of transformation of individuals involved in such research projects both at the individual and group level highlights the inherent transformative element of CAE. The far-reaching effects of such transformation holds potential and possibilities long after studies have been completed.

Although some of the CAE research projects reviewed in this chapter had transformation as a major research goal, we have not seen recorded in the literature a clear model for using autoethnography to effect such actional outcomes—ways in which AE and CAE can be employed by practitioners not only to evoke a response or to contribute to scholarly discourse, but for the express purpose of solving real world problems. This is the focus of the book.

The utility and efficacy of the transformative element of autoethnography has not been fully realized. Given its beginnings in the academy, the design approach and method are well situated within academic paradigms of research methodologies borrowing from specific disciplinary focusses. While useful to those within the respective fields, current models of CAE lack an ease of use for practitioners with an explicit intent of transformation. In the next chapter, we advance the transformative autoethnography model (TAM) as a practical tool where the purpose of the autoethnographic effort is primarily transformative. In other words, we turn the spotlight on autoethnography as a inquiry tool for practitioners to use when the primary goal is to facilitate transformational change at the individual, group and/or organizational levels.

References

Allen-Collinson, J. (2013). Autoethnography as the engagement of self/other, self/culture, self/politics, selves/futures. In S. Holman-Jones, T. E. Adams, & C. Ellis (Eds.), *Handbook of autoethnography* (pp. 281–299). Routledge.

Anfara Jr., V. A., Brown, K. M., & Mangione, T. L. (2002). Qualitative analysis on stage: Making the research process more public. *Educational Researcher, 31*(7), 28–38. https://doi.org/10.31 02/0013189X031007028

Bakhtin, M. M. (1984). *Problem of Dostoevsky's poetics*. University of Minnesota Press.

Bieri, F., Tolstikov-Mast, Y. Gambrell, K., Goerman, P., Hernandez, K. C., Krause,W., Mneimneh, Z. N., & Walker, J. L. (2022). Success in International Leadership Research. In Y. Tolstikov-Mast, F. Bieri, & J. L.Walker (Eds.), *Handbook of International and Cross-Cultural Leadership Research Processes: Perspectives, Practice, Instruction* (pp. 587–602). Taylor and Francis.

Bilgen, W. A. (2018). *Constructing a social justice leadership identity: An autoethnography of a female Jewish Christian social worker living in Turkey* [Unpublished doctoral dissertation]. Eastern University.

Blalock, A. E., & Akehi, M. (2018). Collaborative autoethnography as a pathway for transformative learning. *Journal of Transformative Education, 16*(2), 89–107. https://doi.org/10.1177/ 1541344617715711

Bochner, A., & Ellis, C. (2016). *Evocative autoethnography: Writing lives and telling stories.* Routledge.

Bonebright, D. A. (2010). 40 years of storming: a historical review of Tuckman's model of small group development, *Human Resource Development International, 13*(1), 111–120. https://doi.org/10.1080/13678861003589099

Boyd, D. (2008). Autoethnography as a tool for transformative learning about White privilege. *Journal of Transformative Education, 6*(3), 212–225. https://doi.org/10.1177/1541344460832 6899

Carless, D., & Douglas, K. (2021). Collaborative autoethnography: From rhythm and harmony to shared stories and truths. In Adams, T. E., Holman Jones, S., & Ellis, C. *Handbook of autoethnography* (2nd ed., pp. 155-166). Routledge.

Chan, C. D., Harrichand, J. J., Anandavalli, S., Vaishnav, S., Chang, C. Y., Hyun, J. H., & Band, M. P. (2021). Mapping solidarity, liberation, and activism: A critical autoethnography of Asian American leaders in counseling. *Journal of Mental Health Counseling, 43*(3), 246–265. https://doi.org/10.17744/mehc.43.3.06

Chang, H. (2021). Individual and collaborative autoethnography for social science research. In Adams, T. E., Holman Jones, S., & Ellis, C. *Handbook of autoethnography* (2nd ed., pp. 53–66.). Routledge.

Chang, H., Longman, K. A., & Franco, M. A. (2014). Leadership development through mentoring in higher education: A collaborative autoethnography of leaders of color. *Mentoring & Tutoring: Partnership in Learning, 22*(4), 373–389. https://doi.org/10.1080/13611267.2014.945734

Chang, H., Ngunjiri, F., & Hernandez, K. (2013). *Collaborative autoethnography.* Left Coast Press.

Chiva, R., & Habib, J. (2015). A framework for organizational learning: Zero, adaptive, and generative learning. *Journal of Management & Organization, 21*(3), 350–368. https://doi.org/10.1017/jmo.2014.88

Custer, D. (2014). Autoethnography as a transformative research method. *The Qualitative Report, 19*(37), 1–13. https://doi.org/10.46743/2160-3715/2014.1011

Davis, S., & Linder, C. (2017). Problematizing Whiteness: A woman of color and a White woman discuss race and research. *Journal of Dialogue Studies, 4*, 49–68.

Denzin, N. K. (2003). *Performance ethnography: Critical pedagogy and the politics of culture.* SAGE.

Denzin, N. K., & Lincoln, Y. S. (Eds.). (2005). *The SAGE handbook of qualitative research* (3rd ed.). SAGE.

Ellis, C. (2008). *Revision: Autoethnographic reflections on work and life.* Routledge.

Ellis, C., & Bochner, A. P. (2006). Analyzing analytic autoethnography. *Journal of Contemporary Ethnography, 35*(4), 429–449. https://doi.org/10.1177/0891241606286979

Ellis, C., Kiesinger, C. E., & Tillmann-Healy, L. M. (1997). Interactive interviewing: Talking about emotional experience. In R. Hertz (Ed.), *Reflexivity & voice* (pp. 119–149). SAGE.

Geist-Martin, P., Gates, L., Wiering, L., Kirby, E., Houston, R., Lilly, A., & Moreno, J. (2010). Exemplifying collaborative autoethnographic practice via shared stories of mothering. *Journal of Research Practice, 6*(1), Article M8. http://jrp.icaap.org/index.php/jrp/article/view/209/187

Hargons, C., Lantz, M., Reid Marks, L., & Voelkel, E. (2017). Becoming a bridge: Collaborative autoethnography of four female counseling psychology student leaders. *The Counseling Psychologist, 45*(7), 1017–1047. https://doi.org/10.1177/0011000017729886

Hernandez, K. C., Chang, H., & Ngunjiri, F. W. (2017). Collaborative autoethnography as multivocal, relational, and democratic research: Opportunities, challenges, and aspirations. *a/b: Auto/Biography Studies, 32*(2), 251–254. https://doi.org/10.1080/08989575.2017.1288892

Hernandez, K. C., & Longman, K.A. (2020). Changing the face of leadership in higher education: "Sponsorship" as a strategy to prepare emerging leaders of color. *Journal of Ethnographic and Qualitative Research. 15*(2), 117–136.

Hernandez, K. C., & Murray-Johnson, K. K. (2015). Towards a different construction of Blackness: Black immigrant scholars on racial identity development in the United States. *International Journal of Multicultural Education, 17*(2), 53–72. https://doi.org/10.18251/ijme.v17i2.1050

Hernandez, K. C., Ngunjiri, F. W., & Chang, H. (2014). Exploiting the margins in higher education: A collaborative autoethnography of three foreign-born female faculty of color. *International Journal of Qualitative Studies in Education*, 1–19. https://doi.org/10.1080/09518398.2014.933910 (online first)

Johnson, D. D., Edwards, D., & Gray, P. (2020). Coconstructing counternarratives of African American women faculty scholar-practitioners: A critical and collaborative autoethnography. *SoJo Journal: Educational Foundations and Social Justice Education, 6*, 21–40.

Kitchenham, A. (2008). The evolution of John Mezirow's transformative learning theory. *Journal of Transformative Education, 6*, 104–123. https://doi.org/10.1177/1541344608322678

Lapadat, J. C. (2017). Ethics in autoethnography and collaborative autoethnography. *Qualitative inquiry, 23*(8), 589–603.

Lapadat, J. C., Black, N. E., Clark, P. G., Gremm, R. M., Karanja, L. W., Mieke, L. W., & Quinlan, L. (2010). Life challenge memory work: Using collaborative autobiography to understand ourselves. *International Journal of Qualitative Methods*, 77–104. https://doi.org/10.1177/160940691000900108

Lapina, L. (2018). Recruited into Danishness? Affective autoethnography of passing as Danish. *European Journal of Women's Studies, 25*(1), 56–70. https://doi.org/10.1177/1350506817722175

Longman, K., Chang, H., & Loyd-Paige, M. (2015). Self-analytical, community-building, and empowering: Collaborative autoethnography of leaders of color in higher education. *Journal of Ethnographic and Qualitative Research, 9*, 268–285.

Lund, D. E., & Nabavi, M. (2008). A duo-ethnographic conversation on social justice activism: Exploring issues of identity, racism, and activism with young people. *Multicultural Education, 15*(4), 27–32.

Lyle, E. (Ed.). (2019). Engaging self-study to untangle issues of identity. In *Fostering a relational pedagogy: Self-study as transformative praxis* (pp. 1–9). Brill.

Mainsah, H., & Prøitz, L. (2015). Two journeys into research on difference in a Nordic context: A collaborative auto-ethnography. In R. Andreassen & K. Vitus (Eds.), *Affectivity and race: Studies from Nordic contexts* (pp. 169–186). Ashgate.

McPhail-Bell, K., & Redman-MacLaren, M. (2019). A co/autoethnography of peer support and PhDs: Being, doing, and sharing in academia. *The Qualitative Report, 24*(5), 1087–1105.

Mezirow, J. (1978). Perspective transformation. *Adult education, 28*(2), 100–110. https://doi.org /10.1177%2F074171367802800202

Mezirow, J. (1981). A critical theory of adult learning and education. *Adult education, 32*(1), 3–24. https://doi.org/10.1177%2F074171368103200101

Mezirow, J. (2006). An overview of transformative learning. In P. Sutherland & J. Crowther (Eds.), *Lifelong Learning: Concepts and Context* (pp. 24–38). Routledge.

Mizzi, R. (2010). Unraveling researcher subjectivity through multivocality in autoethnography. *Journal of Research Practice, 6*(1), M3.

Ngunjiri, F. W., Chang, H, & Hernandez, K. C. (2017). Multivocal meaning making: Using collaborative autoethnography to advance theory on women and leadership. In P. Haber-Curran & J. Stroberg-Walker (Eds.), *Theorizing women and leadership: New insights and contributions from multiple perspectives* (pp. 103–119). Information Age.

Ngunjiri, F. W., Hernandez, K. C., & Chang, H. (2010). Living autoethnography: Connecting life and research. *Journal of Research Practice, 6*(1), E1–E1.

Ngunjiri, F. W., & Hernandez, K. C. (2017a). Problematizing authentic leadership: A collaborative autoethnography of immigrant women of color leaders in higher education. *Advances in Developing Human Resources, 19*(4), 393–406. https://doi.org/10.1177/1523422317728735

Ngunjiri, F. W., & Hernandez, K. C. (2017b). Resilient leadership and tempered radicalism: Navigating the intersections of race, gender, nationality, and religion. In J. Syed, A. Klarsfeld, F.W. Ngunjiri, & C. E. J. Härtel (Eds.), *Religious Diversity in the Workplace* (pp. 441–470). Cambridge University Press.

Nicol, D. T., & Yee, J. A. (2017). "Reclaiming our time": Women of color faculty and radical self-care in the academy. *Feminist Teacher, 27*(2–3), 133–156. https://www.jstor.org/stable/ 10.5406/femteacher.27.2-3.0133

Pak, K., Leigh, E. W., & Phuong, J. (2021). Asian American women leaders reclaiming leader identities through collaborative autoethnography. In K. Pak & S. M. Ravitch (Eds.), *Critical leadership praxis for educational and social change* (p. 49). Teachers College Press.

Pensoneau-Conway, S. L., Bolen, D. M., Toyosaki, S., Rudick, C. K., & Bolen, E. K. (2014). Self, relationship, positionality, and politics: A community autoethnographic inquiry into collaborative writing. *Cultural Studies? Critical Methodologies, 14*(4), 312–323. https://doi.org/10. 1177/1532708614530302

Prawat, R. S., & Floden, R. E. (1994). Philosophical perspectives on constructivist views of learning. *Educational Psychology, 29*(1), 37–48. https://doi.org/10.1207/s15326985ep2901_4

Sawyer, R. D., & Norris, J. (2009). Duoethnography: Articulations/(re) creation of meaning in the making. In W. S. Gershon (Ed.), *The collaborative turn* (pp. 127–140). Brill.

Senge, P. M. (2006). *The fifth discipline: The art and practice of the learning organization*. Currency.

Sykes, B. E. (2014). Transformative autoethnography: An examination of cultural identity and its implications for learners. *Adult Learning, 25*(1), 3–10. https://doi.org/10.1177/1045159513 510147

Sztandara, M. (2021). "We are fed up . . . being research objects!" Negotiating identities and solidarities in militant ethnography: Postdisciplinary humanities & social sciences quarterly. *Human Affairs, 31*(3), 262–275. https://doi.org/10.1515/humaff-2021-0022

Taylor, M., & Coia, L. (2020). Co/autoethnography as a feminist methodology: A retrospective. In J. Kitchen, A. Berry, S. M. Bullock, A. R., Crowe, M. Taylor, H. Guðjónsdóttir, & L. Thomas, (Eds.), *International handbook of self-study of teaching and teacher education practices* (pp. 565–588). Springer.

Teasdell, A., Lee, S., Calloway, A., & Adams, T. (2021). Commitment, community, and consciousness: A collaborative autoethnography of a doctoral Sister Circle. *Journal of African American Women and Girls in Education, 1*(1), 7–23. https://doi.org/10.21423/jaawge-v1i1a30

Toyosaki, S., Pensoneau-Conway, S. L., Wendt, N. A., & Leathers, K. (2009). Community autoethnography: Compiling the personal and resituating whiteness. Cultural Studies? *Critical Methodologies, 9*(1), 56–83.

Tuckman, B. W. (1965). Developmental sequence in small groups. *Psychological bulletin, 63*(6), 384–399. https://psycnet.apa.org/doi/10.1037/h0022100

Tuckman, B. W., & Jensen, M. A. C. (1977). Stages of small-group development revisited. *Group & Organization Studies, 2*(4), 419–427. https://doi.org/10.1177%2F105960117700200404

Williams, J. P., & Jauhari bin Zaini, M. K. (2016). Rude boy subculture, critical pedagogy, and the collaborative construction of an analytic and evocative autoethnography. *Journal of Contemporary Ethnography, 45*(1), 34–59. https://doi.org/10.1177/0891241614549835

Wittrock, M. C. (1974). Learning as a generative process. *Educational Psychologist, 11*(2), 87–95. https://doi.org/10.1080/00461527409529129

Wittrock, M. C. (1989). Generative processes of comprehension. *Educational Psychologist, 24*(4), 345–376. https://doi.org/10.1207/s15326985ep2404_2

Whalen, G. C., & Simmons, T. E. (2021). Bonded from brokenness: A collaborative autoethnography on maternal bereavement. *Illness, Crisis & Loss, 0*(0), 1–15 https://doi.org/10.11 77/1054137320988476

Zou, T. X., Law, L. Y., Chu, B. C., Lin, V., Ko, T., & Lai, N. K. (2020). Developing academics' capacity for internationalizing the curriculum: A collaborative autoethnography of a cross-institutional project. *Journal of Studies in International Education.* https://doi.org/10.1177/1028315320976040

FOUR

Transformative Autoethnography Model

Our Story

WHEN WE STARTED WRITING THIS book, each of us had already begun our own journey in answering the question "Should transformation be the goal of autoethnography?" We had pondered the nature of autoethnographic transformation for many years, even entered into debates with colleagues. Looking back at our lives through the lens of autoethnography, we saw clearly the enlightenment and consequent changes that had emerged in us, our relationships, and our surroundings through this work. The process of autoethnographic explorations had altered our hearts, minds, and behaviors over time. The wealth of these experiences and the evidence from the literature were plentiful. Whether we chose to name it or claim it, transformation was an outcome of both the process and products of autoethnographic inquiry. Why shouldn't transformation be a goal of autoethnographic inquiry?

As we were beginning to frame our response to this question, we found ourselves asking other questions as well. If transformation already happens in the autoethnographic process, what else is there beyond acknowledging that innate power of autoethnography? What if we were able to harness the inherently transformative power of autoethnography and steer it towards some desirable goals? If we could do that, what would be the benefits and concerns of this kind of guided transformation? When we met in our monthly book writing meetings to explore these questions, we found ourselves challenged to create a clear process for getting there. It turned out that our journey to get from "Why not?" to "How?" was just beginning.

****

We answer the question "Should transformation be the goal of autoethnography?" with an affirmative "Yes!" We have already argued based on the literature in the previous two chapters and our own research (Bilgen, 2018; Chang et al., 2014; Hernandez et al., 2014; Longman et al., 2015) about the transformative benefit of autoethnographic work. In this chapter we make explicit how the transformative goal can be embedded in autoethnography to interlace the benefits of autoethnography as both a self-discovery inquiry method and a tool of praxis. To optimize the benefits, we offer the transformative autoethnography model (TAM) as a guide.

The TAM reflects an eclectic interdisciplinary understanding of how transformative learning, as a metatheory, occurs (Hoggan, 2016; Hoggan & Kloubert, 2020). Still transformative learning within the TAM is organized around these main processes:

1. Noticing experiences that create a disorienting dilemma or conflict;
2. Critically assessing through self-reflexivity one's experiences and previous assumptions;
3. Grappling with new interpretations and new knowledge through dialogicality;
4. Applying new practices, skills, and knowledge, potentially replacing old views with new perspectives;
5. Evaluating transformative impact and decision making around further actions.

These processes build off the strength of autoethnography as a method of inquiry and extend the reach to praxis orientations.

One might argue that since transformation is a natural partner of autoethnography, there is no need to couple the terms *transformative* and *autoethnography* to create the TAM. However, our attempt is intentional in two ways. By coupling these terms, we not only highlight the natural power of transformation embedded in the whole TAM process, but also offer practical and actionable guidance to autoethnographers who pursue purposeful changes in their lives and consequently in their surroundings. The TAM invites autoethnographic researcher-practitioners onto the path of ethnographic self-discovery that grounds plans for further development and transformation in their personal and professional lives. The characteristics of the TAM are explained in this chapter, followed by a discussion of the TAM's methodological process and guidelines for usage.

Characteristics of the Transformative Autoethnography Model

The transformative autoethnography model (TAM) intentionally channels the inherent self-discovery that emerges in a systematic self-reflexive inquiry process toward autoethnographers' purposeful endeavors of transformation. The TAM takes on the fundamental methodologic characteristics of autoethnographic work. Self-reflexivity, as the core activity in autoethnography, is used to engage inquirers in critical examinations of self in relation to others and contexts in the entire process. The TAM consists of two cycles of actions: (a) the transformative learning cycle, which feeds into (b) the subsequent cycle of transformative application. The results of the first cycle of autoethnographic discovery are used to build the autoethnographer's transformative action plan for implementation. This resultant action plan can then serve as a gauge for intended changes of attitude, knowledge, skills, and/or behaviors. Action plans can be targeted toward transformation at a personal, organizational, or societal level.

As a practical application tool, the TAM distinguishes itself from autoethnography as a qualitative research method in two ways. First, the TAM embeds the intentionality of transformation in the process, especially within the transformative application cycle. Second, whereas the autoethnographic research method traditionally concludes with producing autoethnographic research reports or creative/performative products with possible attendant benefits of transformation, the TAM continues the inquiry process further. The autoethnographic findings and transformative benefits at the end of the transformative learning cycle are applied within the transformative application cycle to facilitate purposeful transformation.

With this foundational understanding of the TAM, the following characteristics highlight its distinctiveness: (a) its continuous engagement of systematic and critical self-reflexivity as its primary inquiry method; (b) its explicit attention to transformation embedded in the process; and (c) its practical application of autoethnographic discovery to subsequent transformative actions. Each characteristic is explained in more detail in the following section.

Systematic and Critical Self-Reflexivity

The entire process of TAM relies on the autoethnographic methodology of self-reflexivity. As noted in Chapter One, we refer to self-reflexivity as systematic and critical examination of the self's life experiences in relation to others who occupied their physical, cognitive, and psychological spaces within a given sociocultural context. This understanding of self-reflexivity discards the possibility that the past and present self can be understood within a self-centered vacuum. Instead, it begins with the assumption that the self's lived experiences are constructed in relation to others within their sociocultural contexts. As Hermans (2001) and other dialogical researchers (Hermans & Geezer, 2012) would argue, it requires autoethnographers to be engaged in dialogue with others within their cognitive and psychological spaces. In some cases, autoethnographers have attempted to embody others in real dialogues to receive help in recalling facts or coconstructing the social meanings of their experiences. This method of "interactive interviewing" was employed by Ellis (2004), Bilgen (2018), and Anderson and Glass-Coffin (2016), among others. Self-reflexivity surfaces the self's connection to others and their sociocultural contexts while autoethnographers "dialogue with others" through recalling, reflecting, observing, analyzing, evaluating, critiquing, constructing, and interpreting self.

Who then are "others" in autoethnographic inquiry? *Others*, in this text, refer to human beings other than the self and could include intimate others such as family members, friends, neighbors, and colleagues, with whom the self has directly interacted, influenced, or been influenced by. *Others* could also mean strangers with whom the self is in direct or indirect relationships or who reside outside of the realms of direct influence to the self but function as anonymous contributors to the sociocultural contexts for the self.

Unlike this classification of others based on personal intimacy, Chang (2008, 2021) typologized others into three groups based on the self's perceptive distance from others' sociocultural positions. The groups include (a) *others of similarity*, who are considered to share similar worldviews and life experiences with the self; (b) *others of difference*, who are considered to embrace different worldviews and life experiences than the self; and (c) *others of opposition*, who are considered to possess the irreconcilable differences from the self (Chang, 2008, pp. 134–135). Others could also wield influences in the self's imagination and memories, as Hermann (2005, 2014) wrote about his lost father. Therefore, autoethnographers can engage their self-reflexivity through interactive interviews with living others as well as imaginative dialogues with conceptual others to examine their influences on the self.

What does critical and systematic self-reflexivity look like? The examination of reflexivity is embedded in sociocultural contexts which shape how the self perceives and responds to others and how the self and others relate to each other. Namely, the intersubjectivity of the self and others is highly contextual. Poerwandari (2021) defines *intersubjectivity* as "entail[ing] the interchange of thoughts and feelings between individuals," compared to *reflexivity* as "the researcher being aware of their effect on the process and outcomes of research" (p. 6). Unlike Poerwandari's differentiation between intersubjectivity and reflexivity, we encapsulate both intersubjectivity and reflexivity as inextricable elements of self-reflexivity in the TAM process. As such, employing the TAM, the self engages in critical dialogue with others in consideration of their relational contexts (p. 6). Inquirers also examine their perceptions and experiences with varying others and the influences of their sociocultural contexts because the contexts shape how the self perceives and responds to others. Therefore, the TAM process utilizes self-reflexivity, anchored on the critically dialogical examination of self, others, and contexts, while examining the past and present self and planning for further development of the future self.

Explicit Attention to Transformation

The TAM process pays explicit and intentional attention to transformation throughout the process. The transformative intent becomes apparent in both the transformative learning and application cycles:

1. Within the first cycle of activities geared toward self-discovery in relation to others and contexts, autoethnogaphers select the focus of the inquiry based on their desired transformation goal/s.
2. Within the subsequent cycle of actions, autoethnographers revise their transformation goals as needed, build out their action plan for purposeful transformation, and assess their further development. These actions are based on the results of the self-discovery from the previous cycle of transformative learning, which serve as a baseline.

As the self-reflexive process continues for the observation of self in relation to others and contexts, the transformative intent becomes clearer and more explicit to autoethnographers as they move from the beginning (i.e., the selection of the inquiry focus and initial transformative intent), to the middle (i.e., the shaping of the transformative goals and development of a transformative action plan), and then to the end (i.e., implementation and evaluation of the action plan) of the TAM process.

TAM inquirers intend to build their action plan for future transformation based on their discovery about themselves. Hence, at the onset of the study, they select the TAM topic and advance a very broad and tentative transformation goal. The intentional attention to transformation, however, should not be misunderstood as sanctioning an intentionally biased inquiry process toward the transformation goal in the exploration and discovery phases. In the preaction phases in the TAM process, autoethnographers are expected to engage the autoethnographic inquiry process as truthfully as possible without "cherry-picking" only favorable evidence, artificially forcing conclusions, or purposefully engineering changes along the inquiry process. Rather, the initial exploration and discovery phases of the TAM process allow autoethnographers to explore their past experiences pertaining to the selected topic and accurately describe the current state of the self in relation to others and contexts. It is through this organic autoethnographic inquiry process that transformation of the self begins. Insights gained through self-reflexivity can then be used to revise/reshape the original transformation intent into clear goals and to create a well-informed action plan for purposeful transformation.

Praxis Orientation

The TAM process does not stop at the end of discovery-oriented inquiry activities. Instead, it embraces a more utilitarian mission to turn discovery into an actionable plan toward further transformation through implementation. Therefore, the TAM extends the benefit of autoethnography as a social science research method into the practical field of development. Transformation that is inherent in the learning cycle becomes targeted and refined in the application cycle as the scientifically discovered findings are directly applied to the lives of autoethnographers and their immediate surroundings.

The practicality of the TAM process is manifested from the beginning through to the end. Its action orientation becomes particularly apparent when the results of the discovery process are shaped into a transformative action plan. At the beginning of the action phase, following the discovery phase, autoethnographers reshape the initial transformation intent to construct transformation goals with an attendant action plan. The action plan leads to its implementation, monitoring of the progress, and evaluation of the transformative outcome. The outcome assessment also becomes the basis for decision-making and further transformation planning or discontinuation of the TAM process. This action cycle enables TAM practitioners to connect autoethnographic discovery to transformative action.

The action cycle resembles the problem-solving nature of action research that starts the investigation with identifying a problem for the purpose of solving the problem at the end (Snoeren et al., 2012). Whereas the TAM benefits from the general thinking of action research for its action-orientation toward transformative goals, it is important to distinguish the TAM from action research. Action research, which originated from systems thinking, attempts to solve narrowly defined close-ended problems of bounded systems (Burns, 2015; Eelderink et al., 2020; Flood 2010; Piggot-Irvine et al., 2018). Conversely, TAM strives to achieve open-ended life-changing transformative goals focusing on autoethnographers' personal contexts.

Here the TAM process has been identified with three characteristics: the intentional attention to transformation as the ultimate goal of the process, the continuous engagement of critical self-reflexivity anchored on the dialogue with others in consideration of sociocultural contexts, and the praxis orientation that combines the exploration, discovery, and practical action for further transformation. These characteristics become obvious in our explanation of varying phases in the TAM process in the following section.

Transformative Autoethnography Model

The transformative autoethnography model (TAM) process undergoes two connected cycles of activities from the beginning to the end (see Figure 4.1). The transformative learning cycle (TLC), consists of three phases of activities: (a) preparation; (b) exploration; and (c) discovery. The first cycle (TLC), particularly with the findings at the last phase of discovery, feeds into the beginning of the second cycle, the transformative application cycle (TAC), which also gauges three phases of activities: (a) planning; (b) implementing; and (c) evaluating.

Although both cycles of activities flow with the intent of achieving transformative goals at the end of the process, the TLC and TAC fulfill distinctive roles in the TAM process. The activities that take place within the TLC assist autoethnographers in taking an honest look at themselves, their relationships to others, and their contextual influences to establish an accurate and realistic baseline for their transformative trajectory for the following cycle of activities. Details about the three phases within the TLC are explained later in this chapter.

A typical autoethnographic research process ends at the final discovery phase of the learning cycle and results in an autoethnographic research product. The TAM process, however, continues beyond the learning process and makes use of insights gained in the first cycle, the transformative learning cycle, to move toward recrafting of goals and application in the second cycle. The primary goal of this succeeding cycle is to expand the impact of the transformative discovery, which autoethnographers started in the learning cycle, toward the direction of purposeful transformation. Therefore, the TAC begins with clarifying the transformation goals and creating an action plan. This is followed by the implementation of the plan and ultimately the evaluation of transformative impacts of the plan. Again, details about these three phases of activities within the second cycle are provided later in this chapter.

Within each cycle, the three phases each have their respective purpose but are interdependent and fluid from one phase to the other as indicated by the double-headed arrows in Figure 4.1. In the same iterative fashion as in other qualitative research, TAM phases could overlap within each cycle so that autoethnographers could move back and forth from one phase to the other. For example, a TAM project begins with the preparation phase of the TLC, which leads to the exploration phase and ultimately ends with the discovery phase. However, departing from the expected forward movement in the path of inquiry, autoethnographers could revisit—amend or expand—activities of the previous phase for better understanding, more information, or corrections of errors. Therefore, each phase is linked to the preceding and succeeding one without firewalls among them, for the purpose of gaining the most accurate and relevant insights about a given topic.

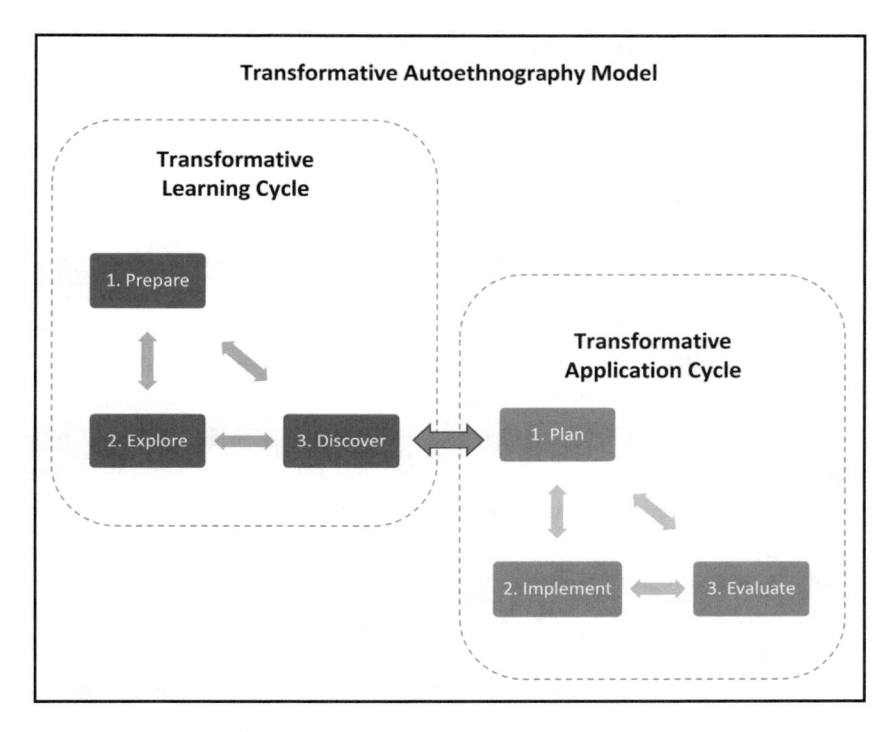

Figure 4.1. Transformative Autoethnography Model.

Transformative Learning Cycle

The transformative learning cycle is the initial cycle of activities in the TAM process. It undergoes three actional phases iteratively: preparation, exploration, and discovery. The preparation actional phase is to select the focus of the autoethnographic inquiry, suggest an initial transformational intent, and design the TAM process for the entire learning cycle. At the exploration actional phase, autoethnographers engage various strategies to gather materials individually and/or collectively that assist them to broaden and deepen their understanding of self, associated others, and relevant contexts in which their lived experiences took place. At the final actional phase of this cycle, autoethnographers analyze and interpret the meaning of their lived experiences as they emerged through the gathering of their autobiographical and related materials as well as the initial transformation experienced through the process of discovery. Autoethnographers focus on their self's relational and contextual understanding deeply and holistically so that they can clarify transformative goals for the next cycle, the transformation application cycle, that are meaningful and authentic.

1. Preparation Phase

The transformative learning cycle begins with the preparation phase. At this phase, autoethnographers set the trajectory of the TAM project, although detailed preparation focuses more on activities for the first learning cycle. In this initial phase of preparation, autoethnographers begin with selecting the suitable focus of the TAM project, narrowing it down to a manageable topic, articulating a broad-based transformational learning intent, selecting the methodological design elements, and setting a suitable time frame for the project. For example, a general focus on "the improvement of cross-cultural working relationships," may be narrowed to a specific topic of "the improvement of cross-racial relationships in my project team." The workable TAM topic is drawn upon the personal experiences of TAM project participants. Since the TAM topic shapes the subsequent course of exploration and ultimate discovery that will serve as a launching pad for their future transformation plan, the TAM topic needs to be selected with the consideration of autoethnographers' transformative intent for further change, improvement, or development. To this end, the participants can set an initial transformative intent, for example: "To gain a practical understanding of how I/we can improve cross-racial relationships on my/our team." Since autoethnography is concerned with the sociocultural existence of the self, possible TAM topics may be found in the areas of autoethnographers' personal lives that intersect with relational and sociocultural concerns.

The selection of the TAM project topic should also be in tandem with the TAM format of either individual autoethography (IAE) or collaborative autoethnography (CAE). Depending on the format of the TAM, individuals or a group of autoethnographers will participate differently in the decision process. It is critical for initiating autoethnographers to align the TAM focus, transformative purpose, and format closely in this preparation phase. Considering the transformative intent of the TAM process, autoethnographers also need to commit to participating in the entire TAM process so that all will experience the full benefit of transformation. Time constraints are always an issue to any long-term project. Therefore, autoethnographers engaged in the TAM process should plan to adjust their process according to their particular time constraints. Once the focus, purpose, and design elements (format and participant/s) of the TAM project are determined, participating autoethnographers design activities for subsequent phases of exploration and discovery and the timeline for each phase.

The initial design is subject to further modification as the learning cycle of activities in exploration and discovery unfold. This design flexibility is consistent with norms for the qualitative research process. Decisions at one phase can easily impact decisions in the following phases and require suitable adaptation to collect more relevant information, and/or to adopt more contextually appropriate analysis and interpretation of the gathered information. In the same way, since activities in the transformative application cycle are shaped by the learning and discovery from the first cycle, the adjustment to the transformative learning cycle could invariably lead to modification of the second cycle. Despite anticipated flexibility in the process, however, more thoughtful planning is likely to enhance the manageability and efficiency of the TAM process. Therefore, a TAM project planning template is offered in Table 4.1 to assist beginning TAM practitioners, with the understanding that the template should be considered neither prescriptive nor restrictive.

2. Exploration Phase

The second phase of the TLC focuses on the open-exploration of autoethnographers' personal experiences pertaining to the TAM topic. From the perspective of the TAM, personal experiences represent the interweaving of the personal and the social. Personal experiences open the door to the understanding of the world where the personal experience was formed and shaped by the self's interaction with others and in particular sociocultural contexts. Positioned as insiders to their own experiences, authoethnographers can engage in a deeper level of interrogation of their socioculturally shaped personal experiences than external researchers.

In the exploration phase, therefore, TAM practitioners can collect their personal experiences through a variety of data collection methods. They do not need to rely only on their memories. Instead, they can expand their sources of information to include others, any previously existing personal or public

Table 4.1. Transformative Autoethnography Project Planning Template

Autoethnographer(s)	
Project Title	
Project Focus	
Project Purpose	
Project Format (IAE or CAE)	
Timeline (beginning-ending):	

TAM Phase	Activities	Participants	Timeframe (from–to–)
Transformative Learning Cycle (TLC)			
1. Prepare	Identify the project focus		
	Decide on the project purpose(s)- the transformative intent		
	Select the project design elements		
	Plan for data collection (exploration and discovery)		
	Plan for data analysis (discovery)		
2. Explore	Collect data: Activity 1		
	Collect data: Activity 2 . . . n		
3. Discover	Review collected data: Activity 1		
	Review collected data: Activity 2 . . . n		
	Identify themes from the collected data		
Transformative Application Cycle (TAC) (Note: This portion may be filled in later)			
1. Plan	Identify/clarify goals for transformation and expected outcomes		
	Connect the goals with the results from the previous discovery phase		
	Plan actions to reach the transformation goals		
2. Implement	Implement the action plan		
	Individually or collaboratively monitor progress and record observations		
3. Evaluate	Review monitoring notes to assess alignment or gaps between the transformation goals and outcomes		
	Evaluate the process and outcome		
	Determine if further action is to be engaged		

materials, and interactive insights that emerged from dialogues with others. Table 4.2 presents various individual and collaborative data collection techniques that TAM practitioners might utilize, e.g., recalling, inventorying, journal writing, and self-reflective writing (Chang, 2008); self-observation (Rodriguez et al., 2002); vignette-writing (Bilgen, 2018); social network visualization (Sathiyanarayanan & Burlutskiy, 2015), kinship relationships such as kinsgram (Chang, 2008); artifact collection (Galman, 2011); dialogical writing (Toyosaki et al., 2009); interactive interview (Ellis et al., 1997; Gale & Wyatt, 2006); and focus group (Chang et al., 2014; Longman et al., 2015). More varieties are listed under the individual data collection category; they are not, however, reserved only for individual autoethnographic exploration. Collaborative autoethnographies using TAM could engage individualized data collection methods to collect individual data separately and then make use of these data in collaborative group activities to enrich the data collection pool.

As previously discussed, the three phases within both cycles—the TLC and the TAC—are not discrete but rather overlapping phases. Given the transformative element that is part of the autoethnographic method, the exploration

Table 4.2. Autoethnographic Data Collection Techniques

Data Collection Techniques	Detailed Collection Plan and Data Types	Data Sources
Individual Data Collection (solo activity)		
Recalling and retelling in story		
Vignette-writing		
Inventorying		
Journaling		
Self-observation		
Visualizing relationships		
Self-introspective or self-reflective writing		
Collecting artifacts		
Collaborative Data Collection (group activity)		
Interactive interview		
Dialogical writing		
Focus group		

phase can lead to changes both at the individual and the group level. As individuals recollect personal data linked to their relational selves, they can experience new insights and shifts in their thinking. Through self-reflexivity, they come to discover things about themselves that might have been overlooked. In the critically dialogic processes of engaging with their various selves in individual autoethnographic work and/or the interactive interviewing of others, they become transformed. This same process can take place in the context of collaborative autoethnographic exploration with the added element of group transformation as the team works to make sense of their collected data in community. In this way, exploration and discovery often work in tandem to move the TAM process along.

3. Discovery Phase

In the third phase of the TLC, autoethnographers turn their collected data into findings through analysis and contextual interpretation. Autoethnographers may use different varieties and modes of analysis and interpretation based on their orientation to autoethnographic inquiry. Some may choose to use more formal analytical approaches, while others may use more evocative or informal holistic approaches. In either case, the role of data analysis and interpretation is to review collected materials holistically and thoroughly to produce a realistic picture of the present status of the self with regards to the TAM project topic. Collected materials, some from their past and others from their present, represent the part of the selves through which autoethnographers can explain how and why they have arrived at their present selves in terms of their worldview, perspectives, values, and behaviors related to their selected TAM topic.

To arrive at the final conclusion about the self, some analytically oriented autoethnographers would begin with reviewing collected data, fragmenting data based on different topical categories (i.e., codes in the qualitative research language), grouping codes by similar content, and transcending details of coded data to identify emerging relationships among fragmented data drawn upon personal experiences. Other autoethnographers who embrace a more holistically interpretive process at this phase may prefer reviewing collected materials while jotting down emergent insights and ideas to organize their discovery. Similarly, those TAM practitioners who opt for more evocative approaches to data analysis and interpretation may choose creative analytic practices (CAP) as one way of listening to the data through writing and rewriting in various ways (i.e., poems or vignettes), each time exploring new depths of the emerging story (Ellis, 2004; Richardson & St. Pierre, 2005).

Whichever strategies TAM practitioners employ, their ultimate findings from this discovery phase work to illuminate the current state of the selves in relation to the TAM project's focus and the relational and contextual explanations about their current state. Table 4.3 presents a worksheet that TAM practitioners may utilize to capture insights, ideas, wonderings, questions, hypotheses, and preliminary findings that emerge while they review, analyze, and interpret collected information. To use this tool, we suggest that autoethnographers organize their collected materials, label each item with a unique identification number, and, if possible, paginate the item so that specific parts within each item can be easily located. As they jot down their thoughts during this discovery process, autoethnographers should aim to connect such thoughts with their collected materials so that their findings are grounded in data collected during the exploration phase. The notes will need to be reviewed, revised, and modified as the analysis and interpretation of collected materials progresses. During the analysis process, TAM practitioners will work to distill these notes by combining similar thoughts and separating distinct thoughts in order to ultimately identify the most dominant, supportable, compelling, and relevant findings. A full discussion of data analysis is beyond the scope of this book; however, we recommend qualitative and/or autoethnographic data analysis resources for further explanation (Chang, 2008; Hughes & Pennington, 2017; Miles et al., 2019; Saldana, 2021).

The discovery phase leads to some sort of autoethnographic product. Typically, autoethnographic research ends with this phase, producing research reports, or alternative autoethnographic products, such as performative pieces. However, in the TAM process, the discovery process does not require a grand research product because the findings from this phase feed into the next cycle of activities for continued transformation.

Table 4.3. Analysis and Interpretation Notes

Autoethnographer's Insights during the Review of Collected Materials	Location of Evidence (Item ID; Page # from the organized data)
1.	ID . . . ; Page . . .
2.	
3.	
4.	
5.	

Transformative Application Cycle

From the initial cycle of transformative learning, TAM practitioners progress to the next cycle of transformative application. This application cycle distinguishes itself from the autoethnographic research because it expands transformative impacts from the learning cycle to benefit not only autoethnographers but also potentially those associated with them and their contexts. The transformative application cycle consists of three action phases: (a) planning; (b) implementing; and (c) evaluating (revisit Figure 4.1). Similar to the transformative learning cycle, these action phases allow autoethnographers to engage their activities in an iterative fashion as they move from the planning phase of developing an action plan, to implementing their action plan and monitoring their transformative progress, to the evaluation phase of assessing their transformative outcomes. At the end of the transformative application cycle, autoethnographers determine whether they should conclude their process or repeat the application cycle with modified transformation goals. Each action phase within this application cycle is described with more details.

1. Planning Phase

The second cycle of activities, or the transformative application cycle, begins with designing an action plan that will help autoethnographers extend their transformative goals. In this phase of the process, the initial transformation intent is revisited and reshaped into clear transformation goals based on the self's relational and contextual knowledge gained from the final phase of discovery in the previous learning cycle of activities. In a typical auto-ethnographic study, the findings at the end of its research process are reported comprehensively. However, the transformation action plan narrows the focus of the findings to establish manageable and workable goals in the beginning phase of the second cycle of activities. In this planning phase of the transformative application cycle, autoethnographers determine which discovery results from the previous cycle of activities are salient to the further development of their personal, professional, or organizational lives, and translate their newly gained insights into actionable goals. Table 4.4 provides a worksheet that will help TAM practitioners construct their desirable transformative goals with expected outcomes by grounding the plan on the knowledge of their current self.

The purpose of this phase is to set a workable plan to steer their actions for change in a desirable direction. The following steps are likely to assist in constructing a successful action plan. First, if working in an individual or collaborative approach to TAM, begin with a goal that is relevant and meaningful to you or the team, based on self-discovery. For example, if you or the group respectively are bothered by relational challenges within your multinational corporate environment and discover that lack of cultural knowledge about

Table 4.4. Establishing Action Goals and Expected Outcomes

Supporting Evidence from Self-Discovery	Action Goals and Specific Objectives	Expected Outcomes

	1.
	  a.
	  b.
	  c.	

	2.
	  a.
	  b.
	  c.	

	3.
	  a.
	  b.
	  c.	

international colleagues and cross-cultural learning habits is a salient factor behind such challenges, focusing on cultural understanding may be a good place to begin planning your transformative application.

Second, make your goal manageable by keeping the focus narrow. Self-discovery can be extensive because it involves not only the self, associated others, and environments, but it also involves deeply rooted cognitive, affective, and behavioral habits and preferences built over the lifetime of the self. As such, it is not realistic to assume that transformation could take place comprehensively within a short timeframe. Therefore, making a short and focused list of transformative goals is a reasonable way to build incremental success toward long-term transformation in a desirable direction.

Third, concretize transformation goals to clear behavioral objectives that can be accomplished within a set timeframe. For example, instead of stopping at a broad conceptual goal, aim for more specific behavioral objectives as follows:

Broad Conceptual Goal

- Improving cross-cultural understanding of my/our project team

Specific Behavioral Objectives

- Instate weekly 30-minute conversations with my/our project teammates from multiple countries focusing on our respective expectations of desirable work conditions;
- Encourage all members to record their observations and insights during the cross-cultural talks for a month; and
- Engage in a monthly group conversation to analyze what to continue and what to improve for my project team.

These more concrete objectives make it possible to easily assess and evaluate outcomes at the end of the action cycle.

Fourth, prioritize the goals and objectives. It is possible for TAM practitioners to discover, while implementing their action plan, that some goals and objectives require a longer timeframe to achieve desired impacts. The iterative nature of the TAM process calls for revisiting, revising, and modifying along the way. In this dynamic process, it may be necessary to set aside other transformative goals to focus on more pertinent ones for greater impact. While such a decision will most likely emerge during the next phase of implementation, it is still useful for the TAM practitioners to prioritize their transformative goals per pressing personal, professional, and/or organizational needs. Careful attention to priority should guide TAM practitioners in making adjustment decisions towards the most relevant transformative goals and objectives.

Finally, articulate expected outcomes. Since the ultimate purpose of the transformative application cycle is to assist TAM practitioners in arriving at a transformed state, the manageability of transformative goals is greatly influenced by their expected outcomes. As shown in Table 4.4, each transformative goal is aligned with the self-discovery result and an expected outcome. Alignment across these three elements helps TAM practitioners track their transformative goals against the criteria of the outcomes. Using the example given in the previous paragraph, the expected outcome may be set as "making up a collective list of helpful cross-cultural insights that the team members have gained and identifying three action items that my project team members will individually work on for the next six months." As the example shows, expected outcomes do not necessarily require any testable quantitative measurement, although a simple evaluation scale with three points (e.g., *achieved, in progress*, and *not achieved*) or more could be developed to help the evaluation process. Such a simple quantitative evaluation plan should be supplemented with rich qualitative evaluation based on evidence from the implementation phase. In sum, expected outcomes should be concrete and specific enough to easily identify benchmarks in the long-term transformative process.

2. Implementation Phase

The second phase of this application cycle focuses on implementing the action plan established in the previous phase while monitoring the process and recording observations along the way. During the implementation phase, data collection is ongoing on two levels. First, at the macro level, individuals or teams should monitor how and if the action plan is being put into practice, manage deadlines, and track the overall time frame. Second, during this implementation period, autoethnographers, whether in an individual or collaborative TAM process, should record self-observations about their cognitive, affective, and behavioral changes. The changes do not necessarily mean that they should record only changes toward the transformative goals. Instead, it will be most helpful for autoethnographers to capture honest and transparent musings about the process, self, and associated others that the transformative action plan evokes. These self-observation records could be as structured and systemized as indicated in Table 4.5 or could be freestyle journals, as TAM practitioners decide. Capturing these data during the process will allow participants to engage in authentic analysis about the TAM process, goal attainment, and modification of future plans that will come after the implementation phase.

To succeed in the implementation of the action plan, it is critical for TAM practitioners to approach this process with a genuine desire for further transformation in their personal and professional lives and/or organizational spaces. To this end, we recommend that TAM practitioners set aside time for plan-based activities and recording, as well as build accountability and support into the process. In the context of a collaborative TAM application project, coparticipants can work as accountability partners through self-monitoring, sharing self-observation, and exchanging insights. However, when the TAM action plan is implemented within the individual autoethnographic format, it will take additional self-discipline and self-leadership in completing the project. Therefore, someone outside the TAM process—such as a family member, a personal friend, or a work colleague—can be engaged as an external accountability partner. In either scenario, it is helpful to establish a habit of regularity by setting time aside for transformative activities and record-keeping for the duration of the project.

The implementation phase may be completed before the next phase of evaluation begins. The implementation phase may also overlap with the evaluation phase in an iterative way to reach transformative goals that are meaningful and relevant to the arenas of TAM practitioners.

3. Evaluation Phase

The final phase of the application cycle focuses on evaluating the extent of TAM transformation. The evaluation criteria come from the transformation goals and expected outcomes which were set at the planning phase of

Table 4.5. Self-Observation Log

Specific Action Plan	Time of the Record	Self-Observation
Action Goal 1:		
a.		
b.		
c.		
Action Goal 2:		
a.		
b.		
c.		
Action Goal 3:		
a.		
b.		
c.		

this application cycle. If practitioners have adjusted the goals and outcomes along the way, we recommend using the most actively pursued goals and expected outcomes.

By the time TAM practitioners arrive at this phase of the application cycle, they will already have experiences with the interdependent nature of the model. Inputs from one phase will be used to build the next phase and to review evidence from the previous phase to make decisions in the next phase. Namely, the results from the exploration phase influence how the next phase shapes up and concludes, and so on. Therefore, in the evaluation phase, useful conclusions will be drawn upon the review of the self-observational and monitoring data collected from the implementation phase.

In the evaluation phase, TAM practitioners review relevant insights that were captured and recorded during implementation of the action plan and evaluate them against set objectives. They start by selecting a rating on the initially drafted rating scale and make additional notes to support ratings. This evaluative work can be done individually or collaboratively. The aim is to produce a summary of findings about how and to what extent each transformative goal was achieved or not achieved and to offer evidence for each conclusion. Table 4.6 offers a tool for such a summary. Based on the final evaluation result, TAM practitioners could decide whether they will conclude this TAM process, revise any part of the process for improvement, or start a new extended TAM process.

So far we have offered detailed explanations and practical tools to guide various phases in each cycle of activities to complete the TAM process. Specifically, the discussion included the prepare, explore, and discover phase of the TLC and the plan, implement, and evaluate phase of the subsequent TAC. Knowing how to do TAM is a good first step in using the model but

Table 4.6. Evaluation of Self-Transformation

Expected Outcomes for Goals & Subgoals	Evaluation Notes
Goal 1. a. b. c.	Achieved: Needs Improvement:
Goal 2. a. b. c.	Achieved: Needs Improvement:
Goal 3. a. b. c.	Achieved: Needs Improvement:
Overall Evaluaton and Future Steps	

may be insufficient for successfully completing the process with meaningful and relevant outcomes. Thus, we offer further tips for the success of the TAM process as well as cautions for potential pitfalls.

Potential Pitfalls and Tips for Success

The TAM draws strengths from the loose combination of three methodological orientations. It is primarily an autoethnographic research method that focuses on the understanding of self in relation to others and contexts through self-reflexivity. However, it also draws on tenets of action research designs through the feedback loop of learning and evaluation, as well as transformative learning perspectives that strive to identify deeper and long-term impacts of meaningful learning. When these orientations—autoethnography, action research, and transformative learning—complement each other, their strengths can augment each other while their weaknesses can cancel out mutual benefits. To maximize the benefits of the TAM process, we recommend that TAM practitioners pay attention to the following fundamentals: (a) the autoethnographic focus; (b) the flexibility of the process; (c) persistent engagement in the process; (d) acceptance of small and incremental changes; and (e) long-term transformative goals.

It is critical for inquirers to focus on the self's contribution to the process. It takes an earnest investment of time and effort to learn about self in relation to others and about the contexts that have influenced the intersubjectivity between the self and others. Encourage all participants to commit to the hard work of genuine exploration for self-understanding by delving deeply into past experiences even though they may have faded a bit or at times be painful or embarrassing to recollect. Inquirers should also remain flexible in the process to allow for the iterative nature of the process, as we have repeatedly stressed in this chapter. Be prepared to stay with the process to the end. Although voluntary participation in a TAM project is absolutely important, maximum transformative benefits are possible if all participants commit to full participation in the process from the beginning to the end. Additionally, we urge inquirers not to become discouraged when outcomes appear to be minimal; instead, acknowledge that transformation is not a one-time event but the cumulation of small and incremental changes. Finally, seek long-term transformation, the pursuit of which in itself is worth the journey.

Other potential challenges exist in learning how to honor multiple voices and perspectives especially in collaborative applications of TAM. In particular, the unique benefits of the TAM process could be hampered when one contributor's dominant perspective works to minimize or silence the perspectives of others in the group. It is important that TAM facilitators work early to set the tone and ground rules for ensuring openness to diverse perspectives within the group. Another issue can arise when the zeal for transformation gets in the way of honest exploration and discovery of current relational and contextual selves as the initial pathway for turning transformational intent into evidence-based goals and objectives. If this happens, the TAM process will not benefit from genuine self-discovery when setting a relevant and meaningful action plan. When the zeal for action dominates the process prematurely without consideration for exploratory autoethnographic self-discovery or the directional purposefulness drawn upon the transformative learning perspectives, the TAM process may be filled with many activities that lead to little significance. To avoid the potential pitfalls of the TAM process, we advise TAM practitioners to guard against the following misconceptions about the TAM relevant to the following: (a) my ownership of my story; (b) my recollection as truth; (c) self-therapy or problem fixing; (d) measuring transformation; and (e) transforming self and others.

1. **Ownership of My Story:** TAM practitioners do not have the privilege of revealing others' life stories indiscriminately although these stories may be entangled with their lived experiences. Autoethnographers should ensure absolute confidentiality and protection of privacy for all participants in the TAM as well as those implicated in their stories through data collection, analysis, interpretation, and action steps (see Adams et al., 2021; Hernandez & Ngunjiri, 2013). In the case of a collaborative TAM project, we strongly recommend that participants strive to practice relational ethics by choosing to act from their "hearts and minds," thus acknowledging "our interpersonal bonds to others" (Ellis, 2007).

2. **Recollection as Truth.** It is important for TAM practitioners to recognize the fallibility of memory data. What we recall or believe does not present the truth. Recalling can easily distort reality to serve the self, and historical happenings could be blocked out of our memories. Therefore,

it is critical for autoethnographers to humbly accept the reality of our own limitedness as we capture our past. To mitigate this ill effect of our limited recollections, TAM practitioners should aim to collect a variety of data that are corroborated by multiple sources to gain a more holistic understanding of the self and others.

3. **Use as Self-Therapy or Problem Fix:** Third, we strongly caution practitioners against the use of the TAM to provide self-therapy or direct problem-solving for personal or organizational problems beyond what the TAM is meant for. In the case of individual autoethnographic TAM applications, individuals facing traumatic life experiences should first seek the help of a professional counselor. In the case of organizational issues, decisions about the applicability of TAM to a particular problem-solving situation should be based on the recommendation and oversight of the organizational leadership team.

4. **Measurement of Transformation:** Transformation is not easily measurable or noticeable shortly after completing activities. Rather, transformation is like slowly aging cheese or fermenting wine. Looking back at significant moments or critical events can provide evidence of incremental rather than rapid motions towards transformation. Change is change whether it is small or great, and whether it occurs suddenly or gradually. It is important to acknowledge that the transformative power and impact is not easily measurable with a one-time administration of inventories.

5. **Transforming Self and Others:** Focus on self-transformation before directing others to change. Although the TAM has the potential to transform a group, the autoethnographic transformation begins with inward change through self-reflexivity, self-analysis, and self-critique. To maximize benefits and minimize fallouts, we wish TAM practitioners to begin their individual or collaborative work feeling less intimidated and more confident.

An accurate understanding of these fundamentals as they relate to the application of TAM in a variety of settings will put practitioners in good stead for optimal use of the model.

Summary

Chapter Four builds upon the discussion from the three previous chapters about the inherent transformative element in autoethnographic work. To this end, we advance a transformative autoethnography model for expanding the benefits of autoethnographic research into the realm of praxis. The transformative autoethnography model (TAM) combines both learning and application orientations for use by practitioners intent on effecting change at the personal, professional, and/or organizational level.

The TAM is identified by three characteristics: (a) its continuous engagement of systematic and critical self-reflexivity as its primary inquiry method; (b) its explicit attention to transformation embedded in the process and outcomes; and (c) its practical application of autoethnographic discovery to subsequent transformative actions. The TAM process consists of two interconnected cycles of activities: the transformative learning cycle (TLC) and the transformative application cycle (TAC). TAM practitioners are advised to move through three sequential but iterative phases, such as prepare, explore, and discover. The results from this first cycle are fed into the second action cycle (TAC) beginning with the planning phase and moving to the implementation phase and the evaluation phase. Chapter Four explains each of these phases in turn and concludes with tips for successful completion of the TAM process while guarding against pitfalls that would diminish the benefits of TAM praxis. Throughout the chapter, we have stressed the importance of the iterative but sequential nature of the TAM, which is critical to its successful application.

In the next chapters, we follow up on this theoretical discussion of the TAM model and method with more practical methodological discussions. Chapter Five and Chapter Six focus on individual and collaborative autoethnographic applications respectively.

References

Adams, T. E., Holman Jones, S., & Ellis, C. (Eds.). (2021). *Handbook of autoethnography* (2nd ed.). Routledge.

Anderson, L., & Glass-Coffin, B. (2016). I learn by going. In S. Holman Jones, T. Adams, & C. Ellis (Eds.), *Handbook of autoethnography* (pp. 57–83). Left Coast Publishing.

Bilgen, W. A. (2018). *Constructing a social justice leadership identity: An autoethnography of a female Jewish Christian social worker living in Turkey.* [Unpublished doctoral dissertation]. Eastern University.

Burns, D. (2015). How change happens: The implications of complexity and systems thinking for action research. *The SAGE handbook of action research* (pp. 434–445).

Chang, H. (2008). *Autoethnography as method.* Routledge.

Chang, H. (2021). Individual and collaborative autoethnography for social science research. In T. E. Adams, S. Holman Jones, & C. Ellis (Eds.), *Handbook of autoethnography* (2nd ed., pp. 53–66). Routledge.

Chang, H., Longman, K. A., & Franco, M. A. (2014). Leadership development through mentoring in higher education: A collaborative autoethnography of leaders of color. *Mentoring & Tutoring: Partnership in Learning, 22*(4), 373–389. https://doi.org/10.1080/13611267.2014.9 45734

Eelderink, M., Vervoort, J. M., & van Laerhoven, F. (2020). Using participatory action research to operationalize critical systems thinking in social-ecological systems. *Ecology and Society, 25*(1): 16. https://www.ecologyandsociety.org/vol25/iss1/art16/

Ellis, C. (2004). *The ethnographic I: A methodological novel about autoethnography.* Rowman Altamira.

Ellis, C. (2007). Telling secrets, revealing lives: Relational ethics in research with intimate others. *Qualitative Inquiry, 13*(1), 3–29. https://doi.org/10.1177/1077800406294947

Ellis, C., Kiesinger, C., & Tillmann-Healy, L. (1997). Interactive interviewing: Talking about emotional experience. In R. Hertz (Ed.), *Reflexivity and voice* (pp. 119–149). SAGE.

Flood, R. L. (2010). The relationship of "systems thinking" to action research. *Systemic Practice and Action Research, 23*(4), 269–284. https://doi.org/10.1007/s11213-010-9169-1

Gale, K., & Wyatt, J. (2006). Inquiring into writing: An interactive interview. *Qualitative Inquiry, 12*(6), 1117–1134. https://doi.org/10.1177/1077800406288631

Galman, S. (2011). "Now you see her, now you don't": The integration of mothering, spirituality and work. In H. Chang & D. Boyd (Eds.), *Spirituality in higher education: Autoethnographies* (pp. 33–50). Routledge.

Hermans, H. J. (2001). The dialogical self: Toward a theory of personal and cultural positioning. *Culture & Psychology, 7*(3), 243–281. https://doi.org/10.1177/1354067X0173001

Hermans, H. J., & Geezer, T. (2012). *Handbook of dialogical self theory.* Cambridge University Press.

Hernandez, K. C., & Ngunjiri, F. W. (2013). Relationships and communities. In T. E. Adams, C. Ellis, & S. Holman Jones (Eds.), *Handbook of autoethnography* (pp. 262–280). Left Coast Press.

Hernandez, K. C., Ngunjiri, F. W., & Chang, H. (2014). Exploiting the margins in higher education: A collaborative autoethnography of three foreign-born female faculty of color. *International Journal of Qualitative Studies in Education,* 1–19. https://doi.org/10.1080/09518 398.2014.933910 (online first)

Herrmann, A. F. (2005). My father's ghost: Interrogating family photos. *Journal of Loss and Trauma, 10,* 337–346. https://doi.org/10.1080/15325020590956765

Herrmann, A. F. (2014). Ghosts, vampires, zombies, and us: The undead as autoethnographic bridges. *International Review of Qualitative Research, 7*(3), 327–341. https://doi.org/10.1525/irqr.2014.7.3.327

Hoggan, C. D. (2016). Transformative learning as a metatheory: Definition, criteria, and typology. *Adult education quarterly, 66*(1), 57–75. https://doi.org/10.1177/0741713615611216

Hoggan, C. D., & Kloubert, T. (2020). Transformative learning in theory and practice. *Adult education quarterly, 70*(3) 295–307. https://doi.org/10.1177/0741713620918510

Hughes, S. A., & Pennington, J. L. (2017). *Autoethnography: Process, product, and possibility for critical social research.* SAGE.

Longman, K. A., Chang, H., & Loyd-Paige, M. (2015). Self-analytical, community-building, and empowering: Collaborative autoethnography of leaders of color in higher education. *Journal of Ethnographic & Qualitative Research, 9*(4). 268–285.

Miles, M. B., Huberman, A. M., & Saldana, J. (2019). *Qualitative data analysis: A methods sourcebook* (4th ed.). SAGE

Piggot-Irvine, E., Ferkins, L., & Cady, P. (2018). Goal attainment scaling in action research: enhancing a systems thinking orientation. *Systems Research and Behavioral Science, 35*(2), 191–202. https://doi.org/10.1002/sres.2459

Poerwandari, E. K. (2021), Minimizing bias and maximizing the potential strengths of autoethnography as a narrative research. *Japanese Psychological Research, 63*(4), 310–323. https://doi.org/10.1111/jpr.12320

Richardson, L., & St. Pierre, E. A. (2005). Writing: A method of inquiry. In N. K. Denzin & Y. S. Lincoln (Eds.), *The SAGE handbook of qualitative research* (pp. 959–978). SAGE.

Rodriguez, N. M., Ryave, A., & Ryave, A. L. (2002). *Systematic self-observation: A method for researching the hidden and elusive features of everyday social life* (Vol. 49). SAGE.

Saldana, J. (2021). *The coding manual for qualitative researchers* (4th ed.). SAGE.

Sathiyanarayanan, M., & Burlutskiy, N. (2015, January). Design and evaluation of euler diagram and treemap for social network visualisation. In *2015 7th international conference on communication systems and networks (COMSNETS)* (pp. 1–6). IEEE. https://doi.org/10.1109/COMSNETS.2015.7098715

Snoeren, M. M., Niessen, T. J., & Abma, T. A. (2012). Engagement enacted: Essentials of initiating an action research project. *Action Research, 10*(2), 189–204. https://doi.org/10.1177/1476750311426620

Toyosaki, S., Pensoneau-Conway, S. L., Wendt, N. A., & Leathers, K. (2009). Community autoethnography: Compiling the personal and resituating whiteness. *Cultural Studies? Critical Methodologies, 9*(1), 56–83. https://doi.org/10.1177/1532708608321498

FIVE

TAM Applications for Individual Autoethnography

I N SPITE OF THE INHERENT transformative capabilities of autoethnographic work and a possible desire for the same by inquirers, intent does not automatically translate into transformative impact or outcomes. In fact, "many narratives are abandoned, silenced, or lost" (Grenier & Collins, 2016, p. 361), partly because the path beyond the autoethnographic product is not well charted. Yet autoethnographic narratives provide compelling presentations of individual realities, capable of stirring the imagination toward problem solving and action (Boylorn & Orbe, 2020; Grenier & Collins, 2016; Miller et al., 2020). The TAM was designed to provide a clear path to help autoethnographic inquirers with transformative intent move beyond revelation, insight, and knowledge creation at the heart and mind level, and into action.

In this chapter we explore how the TAM application might look as it is undertaken by individual autoethnographers. Throughout each case, the focus remains on how the individual inquirer engages the cycles of the model and how transformative learning and transformative action might unfold. As the TAM is applied in these scenarios, the individual transformative impact is highlighted as well the connections between individual and societal change. But first, we begin with some ground rules and considerations that are unique to individual autoethnographic work and the TAM applications.

Methodological Considerations for IAE

In addition to the more general practice guidelines presented in the previous chapter that apply to all autoethnography, here are a few other considerations to keep in mind when doing individual autoethnographic work.

Deeply Personal

Since all autoethnographic activities are situated in a personal context, it can feel achingly close, vulnerable, and sometimes downright frightening to begin to see new realities about one's self and one's social context. The issues that are addressed through autoethnographic explorations are likely ones that individuals are passionate about. These issues will be looked at with intensity and detail, and will involve recall of the past. Such recollections can stir up many layers of emotion. It is helpful to prepare oneself to encounter emotional disruptions and to curate a circle of support which may be needed to begin this work. A useful question to ask in preparation for this kind of work is: "What and who do I need to help me walk this transformative journey?"

Self-care is something autoethnographers often need to cultivate. We recommend kindness, openness, curiosity, and humility as starting points for self-care. Taking an open, nonjudgemental stance when considering all personal experiences and self-observations, whether at the emotional, physical, spiritual, or cognitive level, takes practice. And doing so will expand one's capacity for meaning making and imaging future possibilities for change.

Potential for Emotional Resistance

As much as cognitive disruptions are expected and talked about at length in transformative learning (Ross, 2020), special attention should be paid to emotional responses to these disruptions as emotions provide valuable insight in the transformative process. The process of exploring problems in our life worlds often upsets the status quo and challenges the internal defenses that have kept the status quo in place. Autoethnographic processes often give us access to what was previously hidden. But there are reasons we keep things hidden; our defenses do a good job of protecting us!

We encourage autoethnographers not to waste any emotion by dismissing, discounting, or ignoring it. Emotions speak and offer clues to meaning-making, sometimes even more profoundly than logic. The autoethnographic practitioner should cultivate the art of learning to listen and be attuned to their emotions. This may go contrary to what one has been taught about dealing with emotion in other forms of inquiry. However, in autoethnography, the emotional response to a story is an important mechanism through which we connect to others, make meaning of our story, and see transformational possibilities unfolding.

Relational Vulnerability

The researcher as storyteller should be willing to vulnerably reveal aspects of themselves that will allow for new understandings of their realities (Tierney, 1998). The level of self-disclosure in autoethnography is quite high and raises concerns related to the researcher's readiness and wellness, as well as to the ethics of telling our stories that involve others. Even when the individual autoethnographer is the sole gatherer, analyzer, and interpreter of autobiographical data, autoethnography always involves others. This is because our personal stories necessarily involve and depend upon others.

The firsthand accounts crafted by individual autoethnographers include the relational dynamics within dialogical encounters at the intrapersonal and interpersonal level. Hernandez and Njungiri (2013) remind us that when choosing "to make our lives the subject of study, we have also chosen to make our relationships with others the subject of study," and "the process of studying relationships can change them" (pp. 264–265). The potential for relationships to be altered as they are examined under the spotlight of autoethnographic inquiry should be approached with care, tenderness, and responsibility (See also Ellis, 2004; Frank, 2009, 2013).

Need for Others

Autoethnographic work should be done with openness to methodological input from others as needed. It is sometimes necessary to invite the expertise of others, beyond what is available in a methodological book or article. This may help to keep one from losing sight of the ethno analysis (Winkler, 2018) and getting lost in emotional overload, or simply writing a confessional tale or memoir, which has value, but may lack the deeper sociocultural analysis of autoethnographic work (Stahlke Wall, 2016).

Whereas the invitation for others to join the inquiry process can turn an individual autoethnography into a collaborative one depending on the level of outside involvement (as described in the next chapter), this is not always the case. Sometimes others are asked simply to weigh in on methodological questions, advise on writing strategy, or offer stylistic advice. Being open to the voices of others throughout the TAM experience is beneficial so that the project stays focused, has the rigor desired, and keeps the autoethnographer tied to the dialogicality that is so core to good autoethnographic work.

When one is individually using the TAM, just as in individual autoethnography, one is never doing it entirely alone. In the following scenarios, you will see that each individual autoethnographer always interacts with others in some way, whether through interactive interviews or through the observations and exchanges that occur naturally in the various contexts in which each person is embedded. From our personal experiences with autoethnography we have found all input from others, whether from experts in autoethnographic method, from wise voices speaking through personal interactions, or through the literature, to be extremely valuable as we move through our own individual autoethnographic processes. If attended to, these general guidelines for individual autoethnographic explorations that utilize the TAM will provide a good starting point for inquirers to begin their investigations.

TAM Applications

As we present these case scenarios, we invite you to imagine what you might feel, think, and do if you were to engage with the TAM process. After each scenario is described, we suggest TAM applications, while encouraging you to think of other possibilities for engagement with the model. Each scenario moves through the two cycles of the TAM: (a) the transformative learning cycle (TLC); and (b) the transformative application cycle (TAC). Individual autoethnography sets the stage for the requisite self-reflexivity, critical reflection and dialogicality inherent in autoethnographic work in the first cycle (TLC) that offer insights for the application and action (TAC) that follows.

Within each cycle, there are unlimited possibilities for how each of the three respective phases might be done. As the scenarios unfold, you will see there are many ways to engage with the TAM process. Some scenarios are described using the templates for organizing and planning presented in Chapter Four, but it is not mandatory to use these tools. We hope to show that while the TAM is a guide, it can be undertaken with creativity and imagination, tailored and continuously adapted according to individual or organizational needs. The scenarios here, while for the most part fictional, are loosely based on experiences within different real world contexts in which we creatively apply the TAM to effect potential calls for action in individuals, relationships, communities, and organizations.

Scenario 1: Students Understanding Implicit Bias

As a student in the Master in Social Work degree program, Nomi is preparing for her final field placement work in an agency that processes international adoptions. During her course work, she has been learning about cultural diversity in the workplace, particularly what she might encounter as a human service professional.

Nomi will be doing her field placement at the International Adoptions Agency (IAA). As an adopted child in an interracial family herself, Nomi had considered herself well prepared in many ways. However, some of the readings she has explored during course work over the last year have made her second guess how she feels about interracial and bicultural adoption. She wonders what blind spots she may have regarding her own experiences, and how she can be better prepared to work compassionately and effectively with all people. In her final seminar-style applied research course, students are tasked to examine an issue in which they might experience difficulty responding to the culturally diverse situations they will encounter in their field placements. Nomi has decided to create a project using the TAM to guide her.

Transformative Learning Cycle (TLC): What's My Bias?

Nomi has learned about the transformative autoethnography model in one of her graduate courses and has permission from her instructor to implement a TAM style project to explore her biases around bicultural and interracial adoption. She begins the first cycle, the transformative learning cycle (TLC), by identifying her topic focus around personal bias in her field placement experience. She is ready to begin the three phases of activity: (a) preparation; (b) exploration; and (c) discovery.

TLC Phase 1: Preparation

Nomi is guided by her knowledge of autoethnography that she gained during an earlier qualitative research course. She is drawn to the methodology as she senses she has much to learn from her own story. The TAM project will cover a period beginning at the start of the semester directly preceding her field placement, and extending to the end of the field placement. She anticipates that her TAM cycles will cover three academic semesters, or one full year.

Nomi hopes to answer the general question:

1. How does my identity as a Chinese adoptee to White adoptive parents inform my work as an adoption case worker?

In order to establish the general transformative intent, she considers these two objectives to guide her:

1. To understand how my own experiences may have created biases and how my identity and past experiences may help/hinder my work.
2. To become better prepared in my role as an advocate for children and adoptive parents.

After looking over the course syllabus for her final required course, Intercultural Competence, Nomi is pleased to see that assignments and activities are designed to help practitioners explore issues of bias, privilege, oppression, cross-cultural work, and activities in which they explore their attitudes, behaviors, and biases through reflective and creative writing assignments. She decides these assignments will shape her basic research design, and she plans her TAM project around the course assignments; her course instructor agrees the assignments will offer her the perfect opportunity for the kind of self-exploration and sociocultural discovery needed for autoethnographic work.

TLC Phase 2: Exploration

As the semester begins, Nomi completes the activities in her course that are designed to help students explore their implicit biases as well as how their belonging to various identity categories might impact their work going forward. The assignments are used to help Nomi gather relevant autobiographical data. She completes the Harvard Implicit Bias Test (Greenwald et al., 2015), and the model of multiple dimensions of identity (MMDI) exercises created by Jones and Abes (2013).

As part of the course, Nomi must also complete a reflective journaling assignment in which she is instructed to reflect on the results of her MMDI identity mapping and the implicit bias exercises, with special attention to emotions, thoughts, and new understanding of how her own identities, biases, and position of privilege or oppression might be a factor in her field work context. She is instructed to answer the following journal prompts, which were given in her course syllabus, and which she finds useful:

- Name one thing that surprised you about yourself and one thing that surprised you about how you view others that became clearer through the (activity, readings, etc. . . .).
- Which identity theory from class (Diller, 2018) do you find links most to your identity mapping using the MMDI (critical race theory; Helms's White identity development; intersectionality, other?)
- From a theoretical perspective (ecological systems, symbolic interactionist, communications, conflict theory, etc. . . .) how does this help you understand yourself?
- What does this activity evoke in you at an emotional, embodied level? (Use poetry, music, art or any other literary device that might help you communicate your embodied response.)
- What challenges or disruptions to your identity might you expect in your workplace, particularly as you encounter others whose identities might challenge your own?
- What theories or strategies are you inspired to pursue right now?

In class Nomi is instructed that these activities are being asked so that students might reflect on and critique how they might encounter internal and external resistance and other challenges as they disentangle their own identity-based biases from the larger sociocultural contexts in which they will be working. Nomi is also encouraged by her instructor to find her own voice and mechanism for describing the emotional as well as cognitive reactions that she has to the course activities. This is a helpful reminder for Nomi, as she is a creative writer and often expresses herself well through poetry; she is pleased that this is encouraged in the class.

Phase 3: Discovery

It is often the case that autoethnographic inquiry opens emotional spaces that may not have been accessed previously. Nomi is aware of internal emotional stirrings that she has not dealt with before. She is thankful for the space that she finds in her poetry to express the inner conflict that is arising as she moves through autoethnographic exploration and gathers her discoveries. Nomi includes a short poem in her reflective journal and begins to realize that she had not given enough attention to her interracial adoption before and to the questions that were buried deeply within her around her own identity and the value and dangers of interracial adoption.

Nomi decides to share the poem with her adoptive mother and father and then records their exchange as an interactive interview (Ellis, 2004) based on a discussion of the poem. Nomi shares some additional experiences about being raised in a community of people who look so different from her, as well as the curiosity she has held inside about her own birth story and the culture she was born into. Nomi is surprised by the openness and candor in the interactions with her parents and wonders more openly about her birth mother. She is surprised that her mother in particular has sensed a need to talk with Nomi more openly about this but had no idea how to do so. Through this exploration process, Nomi begins to question interracial adoption in new ways and is noticing a growing opposition to adoption and foster care across racial lines.

For the first time, she wonders if her field placement at the adoption agency might be more challenging than she originally anticipated. She remains open to her own internal responses, the input from her parents, and the course activities that have helped her gather personal insights through both emotional and cognitive grappling with new realities about herself, others, and the adoption systems in which people find themselves.

Transformative Application Cycle: What About My Bias?

Through the transformative learning cycle, Nomi became attuned to potential bias developing in her for same race adoption, and the discomfort she experiences bringing this up with others. And through her poetry, which became an important and legitimate form of data, she has gained a more "sympathetic, empathetic, emotionally engaged and socially conscious engagement perspective" (Saldaña, 2016, p. 158) on herself, the world, and others. She has learned in her coursework that facing the discomfort of preconceived attitudes and behaviors is one way to improve our cultural competence as social service providers. In the next phase of the TAM, which is the transformative application cycle (TAC), Nomi will revisit her original objectives and fashion a plan that aligns with her discoveries, still with the overall aim of improving her cultural competence as a social worker.

TAC Phase 1: Planning

From the discovery phase, Nomi has recognized potential bias against inter-racial adoption as her ambivalence about her own experience has come to light. Nomi has paid close attention to the gaps between what she learned from her coursework that defines a culturally competent practitioner and how her growing preference for same-race adoptions might show up in her field placement. She revises her transformational objectives as follows:

1. To become better prepared in my role as an advocate for children and adoptive parents by addressing my ambivalent feelings towards inter-racial adoptions.
2. To increase awareness in my agency and among adoptive families concerning racially hostile environments that may be inadvertently created through interracial adoption.

Based on these revised objectives, Nomi creates an action plan which includes the following goals:

1. Speak openly with my field placement supervisor about my ambivalence and invite other staff into conversations around my growing awareness of the complexity of this issue.
2. Read other autoethngraphic accounts of interracial adoption and how adoptees and adoptive parents have reconciled ambivalence around looking, feeling, being, different in their family and community growing up.
3. Meet with at least two other people who are part of interracial adoption (as adoptees) and explore how they have dealt with similar ambivalence and tensions; include their input in a handout to support and prepare potential adoptive families for the challenges of bicultural and interracial adoption.

4. Design an interview protocol for prospective adoptive families that addresses readiness for interracial adoption, including supportive material and a conversation starter to be used with prospective parents.

Nomi creates a timeline and sets benchmarks for her progress towards these goals.

Phase 2: Implementing

At this point in the TAM, the initial fieldwork preparation course has ended, and Nomi will implement her plan over the course of her final semester of fieldwork at the IAA. She will have opportunities to carry out the various implementation activities as part of her work at the adoption agency. Her plan is designed to help prospective adoptive families uncover unconscious implicit bias in the adoption process and to work with them to address it. Based on the literature and how her own personal position and experiences in adoption have influenced her, she hopes to become a more authentic practitioner while working with families, and to equip others more fully for increased cultural competence.

Phase 3: Evaluating

Nomi is aware that her transformative goal is something that can be measured both by her own subjective evaluation and through the objective evaluation of her field placement supervisor. Her subjective evaluation includes a new cycle of autoethnographic inquiry to evaluate her own awareness of "what happened (to me, to others, inside of my organizational context) as I implemented my plan?" Nomi plans to keep a field placement journal that is required for her program and will include additional journaling activity to help her track what it was like for her to implement the plan, and what she noticed in herself and in connection with others. As an objective measure of how she changed, she will look to her field placement supervisor to rate her progress toward increased cultural competence in her field placement. With a two-tiered process of self and other evaluation, Nomi hopes to gain a picture of the extent of her transformation into becoming a more culturally competent practitioner.

Scenario 2: Job Satisfaction and Intersectionality

Rita is an English-Spanish bilingual border control officer recently hired at a border control agency that manages illegal migrant and South American refugee issues in Texas. Her department consists of one manager and eight officers, only three of whom have proficient command of Spanish. There are only three female employees, and the department head is a White-European male who used to work in a refugee management agency that primarily served African refugees in Minnesota before being hired by this agency six months ago. Although Rita is of third-generation U.S.-born Puerto Rican descent, the manager has assigned all cases of Mexican migrants to Rita and often speaks about "your people" when referring to her cases. She has begun to feel uncomfortable about her manager's and colleagues' identification of her with Mexican migrants. She is sometimes angry with her colleagues' multicultural ignorance and other times feels discontented with her workplace although she knows that she is a valuable member of the agency. Recently, she has even thought about quitting her job altogether.

Transformative Learning Cycle (TLC): Exploration at the Intersections

Rita has recently done some training in autoethnography and use of the TAM, so she decides to set out on an autoethnographic exploration to discover more about her discomfort in the workplace. Using the TAM processes, she hopes to gain insight into changes she might make in herself that could inevitably lead to wider-reaching changes in her work environment.

TLC Phase 1: Preparation

Rita selects the individual autoethnography (IAE) format because she wants to focus on the way her personal experiences are creating issues for her in her workplace. She decides on the following question to guide her inquiry:

> Question: How do my intersecting identities influence interpersonal interactions, satisfaction, and effectiveness in the workplace?

She has two objectives that help her focus her project:

1. To improve her working relationships with her colleagues around the issues of multicultural sensitivity.
2. To clarify her role and function in helping migrants at the border and gain personal insight that can guide her decision for career positioning.

Rita is guided by data collection strategies she learned in her autoethnographic training and chooses specifically to collect past journal entries and complete a culturegram. Rita chooses to use Saldaña's (2016) invivo strategies for examining her autobiographical data and decides ahead of time to reread her methodology text on invivo that she used in her graduate studies.

Rita decides that she will use a planning table template (See Table 4.1) to help her prepare for her IAE. Below is an example of how a planning table might look as Rita begins the exploration stage.

TLC Phase 2: Exploration

In the exploration phase, Rita decides to use various methods of data collection to better understand how intersecting layers of her identity interact in her workplace. As Table 5.1 shows, she begins by creating a culturegram as a visual display of how she self-identifies. She also makes use of journaling to further explore her thoughts and feelings around the topic, and she conducts interactive interviews with family members and friends about her ethnicity, language, and gender identity.

Table 5.1. TAM-IAE Planning Example of the Transformative Learning Cycle (TLC)

Autoethnographer(s)	Rita
Project Title	My Intersectional Identity and Workplace Satisfaction
Project Focus	Workplace Relationships and Satisfaction
Project Purpose/ Transformative Intent	To understand more about my discomfort at the workplace and the impact of my intersectional identity on collegiality with a hope of improving my workplace satisfaction.
Project Format (IAE or CAE)	IAE
Timeline (beginning-ending):	Approximately 8 months

TAM Phase	Activities	Participants	Timeframe (from–to–)
Transformative Learning Cycle (TLC)			
1. Prepare	Identify the project focus	Rita	Month 1
	Decide on the project purpose(s)- and state transformative intent	Rita	Month 1
	Plan for data collection (exploration and discovery) Rita is guided by autoethnographic data collection strategies (See Appendix B—Table 2)	Rita	Month 1
	Plan for data analysis Using Saldaña (2016) Invivo for theming and coding	Rita	Month 1
2. Explore	Collect data: Activity 1 Use Chang's (2008) Culturegram	Rita	Month 1
	Collect data: Activity 2 Journaling attitude/positions about other Hispanic people, illegal immigrants, this job, colleagues, workplace, etc. (including what, when, where, why, how, etc.)	Rita	Month 1–2
	Collect data: Activity 3 Interactive interviews with family and friends about my ethnicity, language, and gender identity	Rita with family, and friends	Month 1–2
3. Discover	Review collected data: Activity 1 Read/reread data and jot down recurring themes.	Rita	
	Review collected data: Activity 2 Emotion work: Highlighting emotional words in journals that describe reactions	Rita	Month 1–3
	Identify themes from the collected data using Saldaña (2016) Invivo and explore themes in scholarly literature	Rita	Month 1–3
	Make conclusions about the nature of discomfort at work and the impact of intersectional identity on work relationships and job satisfaction	Rita	Month 1–3
	Check preliminary discovery with Hispanic and non-Hispanic colleagues/friends, family members	Rita with Parents, siblings, friends, and colleagues.	Month 1–3

TLC Phase 3: Discovery

Based on the process map in her template, Rita follows the data-gathering steps, remembering that the process is iterative, and that her journaling of emotional reactions, what she notices in herself and others in the workplace, will continue to unfold, even into the next TAM cycle. The TAM process is dynamic and previous steps could alter and inspire next steps, so Rita is not stifled by her plan at the outset. Instead, she is still free to modify her plan as she tries to reach the goal of understanding the dynamics driving her discomfort in the workplace.

Through the exploration of her life experiences and the stories that family members, friends, and colleagues have shared with her about their own immigrant experiences, Rita is beginning to see interconnectedness between her experiences in her role at work and the past experiences of her ancestors as migrants and refugees. As she reads through and analyzes her journal entries, she becomes more aware of her membership in a group that is privileged (she and her family "made it"), as well as a group that was oppressed and traumatized by the immigration system and other structural issues that perpetuate traumatic migrant experiences. This new awareness of her previously unnamed internal struggle has prompted her to read more books and testimonials from others and to create a reading list that she imagines sharing with her family and coworkers. She begins to wonder what role she might have in changing the culture of her agency, using her position as both a partial member of and an outsider to the migrant community. She wonders about what she can do to stimulate awareness in others regarding the retraumatization of refugees and migrants that occurs at the borders, of which all staff at the agency are a part. As she reconsiders her original transformative intent, she feels more motivated to be part of change in her place of work, rather than considering a job change.

Transformative Application Cycle (TAC): My Multicultural Self in Action

Rita's discoveries through the autoethnographic processes embedded within the TLC cycle have given her renewed interest and a direction to channel her energy. When she began the TAM, she was considering the possibility of leaving her place of work. Now, with increased understanding of what is behind her discomfort and the ability to name it as cross-generational community trauma, she is optimistic that she can engage differently with others in her workplace. Now that she has investigated her cultural situatedness from the unique standpoint of cultural insider and border-crosser, she sees that she is similar in many ways to the border crossers her agency is commissioned to serve.

TAC Phase 1: Planning

Rita had identified a disconnect between what she values from her cultural standpoint (openness to those suffering, creating ease for others in navigating the systems of immigration, readiness to be a teacher/leader) and how she is engaging at the workplace. She senses cognitive dissonance between wanting to advance her career, wanting to help the displaced refugees, upholding the mission of the agency and her own best practices, and managing the emotional daily encounters with somewhat hostile coworkers reminding her of her own trauma history.

Her revised objective is based on a recognition of her family's past and the trauma they endured through systems dominated by White bureaucrats similar to those she now works with. She revises her objective as follows:

> To seek and create new opportunities for empathic multicultural exchanges between myself and others in the workplace.

She is crafting activities in the TAC phase in the direction of the changes she is hoping to make in herself first, as well as activities that might prompt change in her workplace. Rita's action plan (see Table 5.2) is based on both internal activity (private, solitary) and external activity (involving others at her workplace).

First, as an internal activity, Rita will use the nonviolent communication model (Rosenberg, 2012) she and her colleagues were trained in as the basis of forming conversations with others in the workplace with whom she has determined there is potential conflict brewing. She decides to gather her emotions, preferences, and desires for the future as an internal exercise. She is not sure how or if she will share her ideas around conflict situations with others. But she is more aware of the need to voice what she experiences in the workplace, particularly with her supervisor, and she realizes through her discovery activities that she needs time to gather her emotions, thoughts, and preferences. Internally Rita is aware that her plan requires that she "lean into discomfort" and "take risks" by emotionally engaging in a different way at her workplace.

Secondly, external actions are part of her plan to involve others. She will invite coworkers to take part in her culture by bringing in traditional dishes once a week to share, and invite them to bring in dishes from their own ethnic

Table 5.2. TAM-IAE Planning Example of the Transformative Application Cycle (TAC)

TAM Phase	Activities	Participants	Timeframe (from–to–)
Transformative Application Cycle (TAC)			
1. Plan	Identify/clarify goals for transformation and expected outcomes.	Rita	Month 4
	Connect the goals with the results from the previous discovery phase	Rita	Month 4
	Plan both internal and external actions aimed at reaching the transformation goals	Rita	Month 4
2. Implement	Implement the action plan	Rita (and others in the workplace)	Month 5–8
	Individually monitor progress and record observations	Rita	Month 5–8
3. Evaluate	Review monitoring notes to assess alignment or gaps between the transformation goals and outcomes	Rita	Month 6–8
	Make decision on concluding the TAM or choosing another project focus	Rita	Month 6

backgrounds. She also decides to offer Spanish tutoring to staff during lunch time. Finally she will invite coworkers to a book club based on the reading list she gathered during her autoethnographic exploration. Through the TLC activities, in particular her interviews with Hispanic friends and colleagues, she realized the importance of sharing her discomforts and not stifling her emotions. She is offering a way to others to walk with her through these issues and hopes this will become an important component of continuous learning and growth for herself and for others.

TAC Phase 2: Implementing

Rita's first opportunity to communicate differently comes with her manager, who continues to seem unconcerned with his language around Rita and continues to use what seems to her to be racist comments regarding the Spanish-speaking immigrants and asylum seekers. She crafts a letter using the three-step nonviolent communication format (Rosenberg, 2012) which clearly states "I felt . . . when . . . I would prefer . . ." in preparation for a conversation with her manager. She notices that doing this helps her process what she was feeling during a specific instance and what she is hoping for in the future. She is ready for this encounter to open a relational space that will reduce the distance between her and him, as that is one of her stated objectives. Her plan reflects her intention for transformation at the individual level in which she is addressing an identified interpersonal issue that is targeted to transform herself. She is also aware that individual transformation can affect the transformation of others when interpersonal relationship patterns change. She realizes that she cannot measure how her approach to her manager will change him or how he relates to her and others in the future, but she hopes that she will notice some changes which she will track in journaling activity as outlined below.

TAC Phase 3: Evaluating

Rita's action plan is meant to purposefully implement activity that will prompt further transformation in the direction that she desires. Self-monitoring and self-assessing progress within this action step can be done using the same autoethnographic methods applied during the TLC phase. She plans to continue journaling about her progress, the reactions to her new way of being in the workplace, and what she notices happening in herself and between herself and others.

At this final evaluative phase, Rita would attempt to determine if progress had been made and if another TAM cycle on a related topic is necessary, or if her TAM process can be concluded. The transformation at the individual level in Rita will likely affect others as she begins to relate to them differently. Perhaps her increased resolve as she begins speaking up more at her workplace, inviting others into discussions and problem-solving activities around her own discoveries, will inspire new actions in others.

Scenario 3: Increasing Empathic Connection

Jesse is a newly appointed clinical supervisor at CommunityMentalHealth. This means he supervises other clinicians as well as manages a client caseload himself. While Jesse is well qualified by education and experience, he still wonders if he was a diversity hire, being one of the few Black and gay therapists on staff. CommunityMentalHealth has a client base that is 50% White, with the remaining 50% of clients from various communities of color, with African Americans representing 25%, and Asian, Hispanic, and Native Americans making up the remainder. Since Jesse has voiced concerns about the underrepresentation of therapists of color on staff, he is aware that now he feels pressure in his new role to prove he can make a difference.

Jesse is also aware that he was promoted to clinical supervisor after a rise in negative exit evaluations indicated that clients at CommunityMentalHealth sense a disconnect with their mental health providers, whether they are social workers, psychologists, or intake workers. Comments on postservice questionnaires suggest an overall sense that clients feel "unseen" and sometimes "patronized" or "misunderstood" by their care providers. Jesse shares a mounting concern with board members and the executive director that clients are not having positive experiences with their care providers, thus impacting the overall quality of care and effectiveness of CommunityMentalHealth.

Transformative Learning Cycle (TLC): How Does That Make You Feel?

In his new role, Jesse decides to make use of the TAM approach to help him become a better clinician and supervisor. Ultimately, Jesse wants clients to be well cared for, and he wants to give good supervision to clinicians who are looking to him for guidance on how to do this.

TLC Phase 1: Preparation

Jesse hopes that in pursuing answers to the following questions, he can help improve the overall quality of care at CommunityMentalHealth, starting with his own practices. His desire for exploration is guided by the following questions:

1. In what new ways can I understand my weaknesses and improve my clinical impact as supervisor and therapist?
2. In what ways might I better support clinicians in my supervisory role?
3. How might the overall culture of care at CommunityMentalHealth be improved so that clients have better response to our services?

His broad-based objectives are as follows:

1. To understand how my personal actions are contributing to the client experience at CommunityMentalHealth.
2. To become more effective in my new role as supervisor as I support clinicians and contribute to a culture of care at CommunityMentalHealth.

Jesse is convinced that as individual service providers understand themselves, their clients, and their contexts of care more holistically, they will be inspired to find better ways to meet client needs, and the agency will see more satisfying, positive health outcomes for clients, as well as a sense of accomplishment among care providers. He decides to use the first six months of his probationary period in his new role to autoethnographically examine some of the issues he has felt simmering under the surface. Jesse is focused on both improving the quality of mental health services he gives and also staying mindful that some negative client experiences may be the result of factors outside of what happens in the therapy office.

TLC Phase 2: Exploration

Jesse is hoping that his training in narrative therapy and his love for self-reflective writing will be of value throughout the TAM process. His exploration activities will help him become more in touch with his own experiences as a therapist and point to areas of practice that have previously been neglected due to the pace of activity at CommunityMentalHealth. He wants to explore his own reactions to client diagnoses, grief and loss, the oppression clients experience, and the vulnerability that comes with seeking help from others. Jesse engages in a series of data collection activities including:

1. **Daily Log of Interactions:** He decides to keep a log of his daily interactions with clients and supervisees that stand out to him. At the end of each week, he reviews his log and uses different color highlighter pens to highlight interactions that he notices embodied visceral responses in himself of any kind. He also jots notes in the margins of his log using one word that characterizes each entry; for example, he writes *empathy*, or *vulnerable, hopeless*, etc. . . . as he remembers what he was thinking, feeling, experiencing during each encounter.

2. **Post Service Questionnaires:** Jesse gathers post service questionnaires that mention him as the service provider. He will use a theming process with the highlighter pens, noticing the kinds of comments clients have made and highlight words that indicate what is present and/or lacking in their therapy experience.
3. **Journaling.** As a daily creative analytic practice Jesse will do unedited journaling for at least 20 minutes in response to the following journaling prompts:

What personal experience comes to mind that in some way relates to the experience you logged with your client/supervisee?

Write about this experience using sensory detail (what did it look like, taste like, smell like, sound like . . . .)

Using emotional words, describe what it felt like.

Who was with you throughout this experience, and what was it like for you that this person was "with you?"

What did you most need at the time? How did you ask for what you needed?

What structural barriers did you encounter when trying to get your need met?

What does this add to your understanding of clients/supervisees with a similar issue?

What comes to mind from your disciplinary training right now?

If you have had a moment of insight, please describe it in detail using whatever metaphor, imagery, or creative form helps you to describe your new insight.

TLC Phase 3: Discovery

Jesse has been able to gather data and identify themes using his strategy of creative analytic practice and highlight themes in his daily log. He notices that his ability for compassionate connection with those he supervises as well as his own clients is often hindered by his own fatigue and anger at the larger systems under which care is provided (i.e., the push to see more clients in less time). He also has become more in touch with his own vulnerability in his new position. He struggles being looked to as "the answer person," often sensing that he does not have the answers; rather, he prefers to arrive at answers in community with others. Jesse notices he often feels a lack of enthusiasm and hope at the end of the day and realizes these are not things he can manufacture for himself, his clients, or those he supervises. He is reminded of one of his favorite encouragements by a mentor of his, "You can only take people as far as you are willing to go yourself," and notes in his journal that his own "narrative therapy process on myself" is necessary if he is to carry out the dual purpose of examining and responding to his own experiences with an eye toward changing the story of how interactions with clients and supervisees might unfold.

Because Jesse does well with narrative exercises, he begins to focus more time on his entries to his daily log of interactions, adding further steps to his discovery activities based on the same methods he uses with clients in therapy. He also includes probing questions in his journaling activity intended to take his discovery deeper, such as:

1. Look at an early entry in your log and create an alternative ending. It is a fantasy ending, a way that you would have liked the entry to go if all the conditions (in yourself and at CommunityMentalHealth) were perfect. This activity is a technique he uses with clients to help them create other possible ways of being in their worlds.
2. If you have had a moment of insight, please describe it in detail using whatever metaphor, imagery, or creative form helps you to describe your new insight.

An important discovery from his logging and creative analytic practice is that he realizes he spends less time with Medicaid clients, because less time is allotted to these clients due to lower reimbursement levels. He has always been troubled by this reality and is realizing just how strongly this impacts his own commitment to serve this group of traditionally underserved clients. He feels ashamed and confused by the realization that the provision of care among clients is so unequal and is based on the source and amount of reimbursement; while he has known this at a cognitive level before, his journaling about this situation daily is bringing his frustration with this reality to a more visible place. He is also aware that the two other Black therapists he supervises feel the same frustration and are looking to him for answers.

Through the discovery activities, Jesse begins to connect his own experiences with the phenomenon described in Maslach et al.'s (2001) seminal research around burnout. While some of the causes of burnout relate to individual stressors and depleted resources for resilience, much of one's experience is "shaped by larger social, cultural, and economic forces . . . that have significant effects on the lives of their employees" (p. 409). Jesse begins to recognize that his burnout experience has roots in his dissonant experiences with the protocol at CommunityMentalHealth that perpetuate insufficient care to some groups of clients, namely communities of color, and specifically those on Medicaid.

He begins to imagine how he might do things differently, paying attention to his journal entries in which he imagines alternative scenarios for provision of care at CommunityMentalHealth. Jesse has reached the end of his transformative learning cycle and is aware of many ways his discoveries can become action points in his action plan. He is unsure which discovery to focus on and is drawn again to the literature on burnout in the mental health sector. The burnout and resilience literature has enabled him to step back and say, "What is this all really about? What's really happening right now, and what can I do about it?"

Transformative Application Cycle (TAC): I Can Feel You

In formulating the transformative action cycle, Jesse draws on burnout literature among practitioners belonging to marginalized groups. His discoveries lead him to focus on the subtle microaggressions in his workplace and the emotional overwhelming he often experiences but diminishes through denial and minimization. Jesse becomes more aware that being one of the only African American therapists, and the only openly gay therapist, has added to his internal hypervigiliance and perfectionism at work; this is depleting him. Based on his exploration and discoveries, he draws on the burnout literature, particularly as it relates to African American experiences, as he formulates a plan around self-care (Menakam, 2021). He sees a direct connection between feeling depleted in his role as therapist and clinical supervisor and his reduced capacity to engage with clients, other therapists, and the administrators of CommunityMentalHealth. He revises his earlier objectives, to a more refined and focused plan around self-care in order to improve his capacity and resilience in his therapy practice and in his new role as supervisor.

TAC Phase 1: Planning

Because Jesse began to realize that his own burnout was a factor in how clients and supervisees were experiencing him, Jesse chooses to focus on two aspects of his practice: self-care and staff support. He revises his objectives as follows:

> Objective: To engage in ongoing self-care practices that will help me effectively deal with burnout so I can better serve clients at Community MentalHealth.

> Objective: To engage in activities that increase my empathic responsiveness to clinicians and clients in my new role as supervisor so that I effectively contribute to creating a culture of care at CommunityMentalHealth.

For his self-care plan he will:

1. Begin each day with mindfulness activities including 15 minutes of yoga stretching at work in the community room. He will invite other staff to join him, but will be careful to communicate that this is totally optional.
2. Continue to journal, write poetry, and draw in his journal for 15 minutes at the end of each day. He has found this helps him identify both troubling and sustaining emotions and experiences that are often lost in the busyness of the day.

In order to increase his empathic responsiveness to clients and supervisees, his plan entails:

1. Begin weekly one-hour focus group sessions designed for therapists to share their experiences, joys, challenges, new ideas, etc. In these sessions, he will assume the role of participant, not supervisor or leader. He hopes to build a space where therapists will freely share without the sense that

they are being evaluated. Rather, he hopes for a more collaborative and open structure to idea sharing, something he realizes he misses.

2. Schedule 1.5 hours for each client (instead of 1 hour), regardless of client's reimbursement source. He hopes this will enable more time to be spent with all clients, and an increased ability to prepare for the next client without feeling rushed.

He concludes his planning session by reviewing his action items and commits to being flexible with the timeline, given his knowledge of the current workload demands at CommunityMentalHealth. He plans to revisit and revise the timeline as needed.

TAC Phase 2: Implementing

Jesse begins implementing his self-care activities immediately. During his mindfulness activity, he was inspired to prepare a letter drafted to the board of directors related to client load and the pressures he and other therapists have felt. In the letter, Jesse suggests changes to scheduling, pay, and streamlined documentation that may free up some of the time therapists spend documenting and preparing invoices. Jesse informs the board he has begun his own "pilot project" and shares his TAC plan, explaining how he hopes his suggestions create a more relaxed and healing atmosphere during client sessions. He takes responsibility for his part in the burnout by tending to self-care, but also addresses the systemic problems discovered during the TLC portion of the TAM.

TAC Phase 3: Evaluate

At the end of the six-month period, Jesse gathers his exit interviews for the period since he began implementing his plan. He decides to use the same methods of data gathering to notice changes in himself and in his clients' reactions to him as reported in their surveys. Jesse also keeps a new log of interactions, this time including a self-evaluation of self-changes form. He tracks what he notices in much the same way he did in the exploration step of the TLC cycle (see Table 5.3). He is considering suggesting this as a self-evaluation process for those he supervises.

At the end of the six-month period, Jesse asks clinicians if they want to continue the focus group or change it in any way. He has them each complete a short survey asking if/how this group time has been helpful and if there is anything they would like to see discussed. Based on the evaluations, Jesse will determine if the focus groups will continue, as well as decide whether to conclude the TAM or continue into another cycle of discovery and planning.

Finally, Jesse explores the updated client surveys as a baseline to determine if client outcomes confirm or disconfirm the progress; he wants to know if clients are feeling more seen, connected, heard, and if they are having positive encounters with him. Jesse notes that, since participating in the TAM over the last six months, he has increased enthusiasm for work and wonders if it is the TAM that has changed him or his new role as supervisor that has empowered him to imagine new ways of being at work. Jesse is experiencing the opposite of burnout, which is engagement characterized by "energy, involvement, and efficacy" (Maslach et al., 2001, p. 416) at work.

Table 5.3. Jesse's Self-Evaluation of Self-Changes

Desired Change	New Behavior Implemented	Date Attempted	How Did It Go?
I will connect with their pain	It makes sense you feel that way because	6/20/2021	This was really effective. I began to notice that their pain did make sense, and I was more invested in helping them find solutions
I will communicate that I am listening	Word for word repetition (mirroring) of last sentence	7/13/2021	Client seemed a little irritated at first, then we laughed when she said I sounded like a parrot. I noticed the laughter did much to "connect" us
Equality of care (no matter the source of payment or the client situation)	Engage mindfully about bias and potential for different treatment of clients	daily	Awareness increased that I had internal reactions to certain clients, and the kinds of issues they presented. Facing this lessened its power and prompted me to address the emotional distance I was maintaining, likely a sign of burnout
Attention to Self-Care	Resumed mindfulness practices which included deep breathing and yoga	Daily	Noticeable decrease in agitation and anxiety in the workplace. More capacity to express

Overall Evaluation and Future Steps
Some strategies worked well, and began to feel natural. I saw that strategies were helpful, but the clients really wanted genuine care; listening and empathizing are paths toward that care. I will continue to use these strategies, even when it feels unnatural, or if our time is running out. Mindfulness will continue to be part of my daily routine. As I am more aware of what triggers my anxiety at work (impatience, pressure, my own stressor) I can attend to how my presence impacts clients more intentionally.

Different Paths to Transformation in IAE

The scenarios we shared show possible paths toward further transformation that originated in autoethnographic self-reflexive processes. Irrespective of contexts, the activities within the transformative learning cycles (TLC) provide a clear pathway for individuals to explore their personal stories through autoethnographic inquiry. These explorations can help inquirers expose their own blind spots and identify gaps between personal values, aspirations, and the social realities that dictate how they actually experience themselves and others, and how they live their lives. The discoveries made provide a critical bridge to the transformative action cycle (TAC) as individuals are better equipped with new insights and understanding about themselves and others that can move them toward actions for even deeper transformation.

Summary

In this chapter we have provided scenarios of applications of the TAM as done by individual autoethnographers. We have done so primarily for illustrative purposes. In practice, these applications would no doubt be impacted by many other variables that are not fully represented here, and that could derail or frustrate a clear path to transformational goals. This is true for any change efforts. We acknowledge that these are somewhat idealized portraits of the TAM at work. In reality, change is messy in practice.

At the same time, we have presented these scenarios to highlight that in individual autoethnographic explorations that make use of the TAM, the self is the starting point that can shape the spaces that we share with others in our communities, organizations, and society. In each case, the individual is positioned as the expert of their own story, with access to embedded and embodied knowledge about themselves and how they work. The individual is able to recognize where self-interest, power, and politics in the larger systems factor into what is possible for future change efforts. In short, autoethnographic processes within the TAM celebrate individual agency as the necessary beginning point for individual, collective, and societal transformation. Individuals using the TAM are choosing to orient themselves to holistic ways of knowing, with their feelings, desires, needs, and intellect, all in the interest of transformative change. Beginning with themselves, they embrace the reality that self-change is the necessary starting point, but certainly not the ending point, for further community and societal transformation.

References

Boylorn, R. M., & Orbe, M. P. (Eds.). (2020). *Critical autoethnography: Intersecting cultural identities in everyday life.* Routledge.

Diller, J. V. (2018). *Cultural diversity: A primer for the human services* (6th ed.). Cengage Learning.

Ellis, C. (2004). *The ethnographic I: A methodological novel about autoethnography.* Rowman Altamira.

Frank, A. W. (2009). Why I wrote . . . The wounded storyteller: A recollection of life and ethics. *Clinical Ethics, 4*(2), 106–108 . https://doi.org/10.1258/ce.2009.009014

Frank, A. W. (2013). *The wounded storyteller: Body, illness, and ethics.* University of Chicago Press.

Greenwald, A. G., Banaji, M. R., & Nosek, B. A. (2015). *Statistically small effects of the Implicit Association Test can have societally large effects.* https://psycnet.apa.org/record/2014-48911-001

Grenier, R. S., & Collins, J. C. (2016). "Man, have i got a story for you": Facilitated autoethnography as a potential research methodology in human resource development. *Human Resource Development Review, 15*(3), 359–376. https://doi.org/10.1177/1534484316656658

Hernandez, K. C., & Ngunjiri, F. W. (2013). Relationships and communities. In T. E. Adams, C. Ellis, & S. Holman Jones (Eds.), *Handbook of autoethnography* (pp. 262–280). Left Coast Press.

Jones, S. R., & Abes, E. S. (2013). *Identity development of college students: Advancing frameworks for multiple dimensions of identity.* John Wiley & Sons.

Maslach, C., Schaufeli, W. B., & Leiter, M. P. (2001). Job burnout. *Annual Review of Psychology, 52*(1), 397. https://doi.org/10.1146/annurev.psych.52.1.397

Menakem, R. (2021). *My grandmother's hands: Racialized trauma and the pathway to mending our hearts and bodies.* Penguin.

Miller, R., Liu, K., & Ball, A. F. (2020). Critical counter-narrative as transformative methodology for educational equity. *Review of Research in Education, 44*(1), 269–300. https://doi.org/10.3102/0091732X20908501

Rosenberg, M. (2012). *Living nonviolent communication: Practical tools to connect and communicate skillfully in every situation.* Sounds True.

Ross, S. L. (2020). A Concept Analysis of the Form that Trans-forms as a Result of Transformation. *International Journal of Psychological Studies, 12*(2), 52. Routledge.

Saldaña, J. (2016). *The coding manual for qualitative researchers* (3rd ed.). SAGE.

Stahlke Wall, S. (2016). Toward a moderate autoethnography. *International Journal of Qualitative Methods, 15*(1), 1–9. https://doi.org/10.1177/1609406916674966

Tierney, W. G. (1998). Life history's history: Subjects foretold. *Qualitative inquiry, 4*(1), 49–70. https://doi.org/10.1177/107780049800400104

Winkler, I. (2018). Doing autoethnography: Facing challenges, taking choices, accepting responsibilities. *Qualitative Inquiry, 24*(4), 236–247. https://doi.org/10.1177/1077800417728956

SIX

TAM Applications for Collaborative Autoethnography

A S WITH INDIVIDUAL AUTOETHNOGRAPHY, MANY opportunities exist for the application of a collaborative approach using the TAM in a variety of contexts and situations. In academia, groups of autoethnographic inquirers often choose to investigate a phenomenon based on similar interests and/or their mutual research agendas. Groups of practitioners may likewise use autoethnography based on common interests around a given topic. However, one of the most potent benefits of a collaborative approach to autoethnography is that it has potential to bridge relational divides through its critical dialogic capacity, applications of multivocality, generative learning, and search for negotiated meaning. The result can be profound transformation for individual participants, the inquiry group, and ultimately the contexts they inhabit.

In this chapter we share three possible scenarios of how the TAM model can be used to effect these kinds of outcomes, as well as provide practical guidelines and resources for practitioners intent on utilizing the TAM in group applications. In the previous chapter, we went into more specific detail at the individual level about possible scenario outcomes. In this chapter, we adopt a more general exploration, first because in collaborative autoethnography (CAE) there is room for group input regarding project progress and timeline. We also offer a more general framework to allow readers opportunities to think creatively about specific next steps under the different phases in the transformative learning and transformative application cycles. But we begin with methodological considerations for CAE applications employing the TAM.

Methodological Considerations for CAE

Before launching a TAM project, it is important to be attentive to best practices and other considerations surrounding this kind of work. The following are suggested best practices when applying the TAM in collaborative work.

Size Matters

At the onset, the TAM leader and participants need to make critical decisions about the group size. While we do not have a specific recommendation with respect to the appropriate size for a particular study, we note that larger groups require more logistical management and can slow down the process or burden it with copious amounts of data to winnow. As mentioned earlier, CAE groups can be very large, with as many as 17 participants (Hernandez & Longman, 2020), or quite small, involving only 2 members. Size considerations should be weighed relative to the resources available to the team, the ability to manage the logistics of a large team, and how much time the group has at their disposal.

Length of the Study

During the TAM preparation stage, groups should create a tentative timeline for completion. Change efforts can take a long time and be almost never-ending. If projects drag out indefinitely, group attrition can be a challenge. Holding in tension the time needed to encourage change and the time that participants can consistently devote to this, team members under the lead of the TAM coordinator/leader can agree to some boundaries at the onset so that individuals can decide whether they want to participate or not. The duration of the project and the expected time investment should be articulated at the onset. Commitment to the project for a month or more is most likely a reasonable framework to begin with, depending on the change level expected. For projects that extend beyond a month, it will be important to set benchmark goals and accomplishments along the way to sustain interest and motivation. For example, in the discovery phase of TAM, participants can be given the option to share their individual progress in public or other forums.

Ownership of Data

As with any autoethnographic project, TAM work can produce copious amounts of data from participants who may be geographically distanced from each other. In some cases, when individuals may not even live in the same locale, TAM projects can be completed virtually. Depending on the length of the study, participants may relocate while the study is in progress. In such cases, care should be taken at the start of the project to outline how the data will be used and by whom. Important questions that can drive decision-making along these lines might include the following:

1. Can any participant(s) use the data to create reports and presentations post investigation?
2. Should all group members be credited for public work reports, workshops, etc., that emanate from the collective data, irrespective of their role in the work of contributing to the deliverable?
3. Will all participants have access to ownership of the data post TAM exploration? If not, what are the agreed-upon boundaries/guidelines for ownership and access?
4. Should all participants have the right to veto the sharing of their autobiographical excerpt or data in a deliverable for public dissemination?

We encourage groups to discuss and consider the issue of ownership of the data carefully, setting clear and agreed-upon guidelines at the onset of the TAM project.

Protecting Individuals

As mentioned many times in this book, although autoethnography celebrates the use of telling our stories for insight and change, our stories are not exclusively ours to tell. Autobiographical recollections will inevitably involve relations with others. Autoethnographers must attend to strategies for protecting the rights of those who are unwittingly implicated in their stories. Wherever possible, we recommend that participants seek the consent of all those who are in their stories. Though not a research requirement, this conforms to relational ethics—we have a human responsibility to care for people and the relationships we have with them. When this is not possible, there are a variety of strategies that can be employed to protect the identity of others involved in our stories, including fictionalizing the story, using an amalgam or composite characters, and even changing a few demographic details that do not change the meaning of the experience (see Hernandez and Ngunjiri, 2013 for more strategies).

Another important consideration is to care for the rights and relationships of the participants in the TAM project. Participants should be required at the onset to agree to keep in confidence autobiographical exchanges shared in the group. In some cases, it might be wise to discuss and create a list of agreements to which participants sign off on at the start of the project. Along with the normative expectations for social science research, this agreement should also inform participants that they have the right to withdraw from the TAM exploration and/or make decisions about which parts of their work can be shared or not shared in a public setting without consequence. In sum, care should be taken to protect the relationship at the center of a TAM project.

Though not an extensive list, these four methodological considerations are located in best practice when conducting any kind of inquiry involving people. Even beyond simple adherence to best practices in the field, however, these considerations value and protect the relationships that are inherent in the personal experiences comprising primary data in autoethnographic work.

TAM Applications

With careful attention paid to methodological considerations discussed above, the TAM model can be used in a variety of contexts using a collaborative approach to autoethnography. Following are three possible scenarios, as well as general guidelines about how these might unfold using the TAM model to effect transformation at various levels. We offer these as a starting point for practitioners to envision the scope of TAM and to stimulate the imagination around possible ways it might be applied in real world situations.

Scenario #1: Educational Zoom Fatigue

When schools shut down all over the world in an effort to curb the spread of the COVID-19 virus, parents and teachers were under great stress. In the Brower County School District, the superintendent had become aware of the concerns through communications with frustrated principals, teachers, and parents. It seemed as though nobody was happy with the current state of affairs. Principals were overwhelmed with securing the technology, training, and needed expertise to facilitate effective online education. Teachers who had not previously facilitated online instruction for a class, or even received much training in using virtual learning platforms, found themselves having to learn a slew of new skills. Parents and students were also overwhelmed with what was expected of them and this new approach to schooling.

While some onboarding workshops and resources provided by principals and the district level administration were proving to be helpful, teachers, parents and students were still struggling. Teachers were complaining that the administration did not fully understand what it was like to effectively teach kids in an online setting. Parents were being challenged to understand how to handle the online learning platforms, supervise their children with this new approach to schooling, and manage both home and work. At times the instructions parents received from the school and teachers seemed haphazard and ill conceived. Parents with younger children wondered if teachers really understood what it would require to keep an energetic elementary-aged child engaged in academics via online learning.

The Transformative Learning Cycle: Educational Zoom Fatigue

School district personnel realized that this transition was not going well. Based on the reports they were getting from principals, teachers, and parents, it was clear that current approaches to online learning were not working effectively to foster teaching and learning. Linda, the school district community liaison, had recently completed a professional development training course in use of TAM. She suggested to her supervisor that this might be an opportune time to use the model to address this case. He agrees and appoints her the project manager to lead this effort over the next three months. To support her efforts, he offers her the help of two other project assistants.

TLC Phase 1: Preparation

Linda sets up a preparation meeting with her team. In this first preparation meeting, they work to set the focus and scope of the project and arrive at the following overarching question:

> In what ways are the use of virtual technologies creating teaching and learning challenges and opportunities for principals, teachers, and parents?

Looking at this question, they are convinced that a collaborative autoethnographic approach employing the TAM would work well to draw out the concerns of various stakeholders. Using the TAM planning template (See Table 4.1), they begin working their way through important steps in preparation. They decide to recruit a diverse pool of stakeholders (principals, vice-principals, teachers, and parents) to be a part of the TAM exploration to better understand the issues around using virtual technologies in education. In their recruitment strategies, they are clear to volunteers that the project is expected to last for three months.

Drawing on the agreed-upon research question, the team then specifies two broad study objectives. The first objective addresses the deeper understanding of the targeted topic, in this case the "use of virtual technologies in teaching and learning." The second objective is broadly targeted at the personal, group, and/or organizational/institutional level transformation which Linda and the team hope will be outcomes from the communal interrogation. These are as follows:

1. To understand the ways in which the use of virtual technologies is creating teaching and learning challenges and opportunities for principals, teachers, and parents.
2. To utilize perspective taking and group knowledge of the use of virtual technologies in education to effect better teaching and learning outcomes for stakeholders.

Linda and the team realize that they also need to make decisions about what kind of CAE design they will use. They review a variety of CAE designs in the literature (see Chang, 2008; Chang et al., 2013) and decide on their approach. They plan to use a concurrent CAE design approach, in which data are collected simultaneously from participants. They will first use an open-ended survey to gauge stakeholders' needs. Based on these data, they will formulate questions for follow-up focus group sessions. At the end of the transformative learning cycle, they also plan to have participants complete an exit survey.

To begin the process, they liaise with principals and parent/teacher groups to recruit a pool of participants, including three principals, five teachers, and five parents. Even though this group is on the larger side for use of the TAM, given the resources at their disposal and the fact that they want to have input from a broad cross-section of the target population, they agree that this number is manageable and likely to yield rich data.

TLC Phase 2: Exploration

The team begins to collect data aligned to the broad-based objectives outlined in the preparation phase. In the first step of exploration, the sample of principals, teachers, and parents are asked to respond independently to the targeted prompts in an open-ended survey as follows:

1. Describe with the use of a specific example what has been the most frustrating thing to you about using virtual technologies in teaching and learning during this time.
2. Describe with the use of a specific example what has been one of the most positive things for you about using virtual technologies in teaching and learning during this time.
3. What is one thing you wish teachers, parents, school administrators knew about the challenges and/or opportunities you face using virtual technologies in teaching and learning during this time?

In the second step, the participants are asked to write responses to the same writing prompts, but from the perspective of others in the group.

1. Describe what you think might have been one of the most frustrating things for stakeholders other than yourself about using virtual technologies in teaching and learning during this time.
2. Describe what you think might have been one positive thing for stakeholders other than yourself about using virtual technologies in teaching and learning during this time.

In the third step of exploration, Linda and her team collate the responses and distribute them among participants for reading and formulating probing questions for follow-up discussions. Taking into consideration relational ethics in this study, Linda asks participants if they would prefer to have their responses anonymized for group sharing. Everyone wants to be identified with their script, so Linda and her team opt to keep identifying information on scripts.

Scripts are circulated among participants as follows: Parents receive scripts that came from principals and teachers, principals receive scripts that came from teachers and parents, and teachers receive scripts that came from principals and parents. Linda instructs participants to read over the transcripts and include questions and/or comments to be addressed in a follow-up focus group meeting the following week. Linda and the team end up doing two iterations of the follow-up focus group and reach a point of saturation—more probing questions are not yielding any new data. Linda realizes that it is time to move to the final step of exploration. She invites participants to write reflection responses to the following prompts:

1. In what ways were your initial ideas about the experiences of others using technology for learning confirmed/not confirmed through this process?
2. What, if anything, do you now know about the experiences of others using technology for learning that you did not know before?
3. What changes, if any, would you like to make going forward as a result of this learning experience?

TLC Phase 3: Discovery

In preparation for the discovery phase, Linda reviews what she knows about best practices for data coding and reduction by consulting the work of Braun and Clarke (2006) and Bryman (2015). She becomes clearer about how to approach the discovery phase of the project and decides to invite the entire group to a working lunch gathering to revisit the starting research question:

1. In what ways is the use of virtual technologies creating teaching and learning challenges and opportunities for me/others?

Before the meeting, she works with her team to collate and summarize the essential points that emerged from the exploration phase. She knows that she needs to keep this concise and easy to read, so she prepares a four-page summary and distributes it to the group one week prior to the event for them to read.

At the lunch gathering, she divides the larger group into smaller teams, and asks them to reflect on the collected data and the summarized report so as to identify and agree on five to seven major discoveries based on the group's exploration efforts. After teams have engaged in this independent meaning making, Linda reconvenes the larger group. Over lunch, they discuss and negotiate the final themes that have emerged. Since Linda is also interested in personal and group level changes, she concludes the meeting by informing participants that she would like them to complete an exit survey and return it to her office the next week. The survey is designed to elicit the following kinds of data from participants to focus on transformation that might be experienced at each of the following levels:

> **Personal Level:** Examine your initial writing at the start of the project. In what ways has your thinking changed, if at all, through this process?
>
> **Group Level:** Reflect on the first meeting of the group to the last meeting. In what ways, if at all, do you think the group changed through the process of listening to and learning from each other's perspective about online education?
>
> **Community Level:** How might our shared experiences and discoveries be used to guide changes within the wider school context?

To encourage participants to complete and return the survey on time, Linda offers a lottery incentive of an Amazon gift card for entries returned by the set date.

The Transformative Application Cycle: Addressing Educational Zoom Fatigue

After the transformative learning cycle, the group now moves on to the transformative application cycle. This is where the insights and changes which occurred at the individual and group level are leveraged to effect ongoing internal changes at the individual and group level, as well as changes within the organizational and/or institutional contexts. There are three phases in this process.

TAC Phase 1: Planning

Based on what was learned in the discovery phase, Linda and her team now revisit the transformational objectives that were stated at the onset of the study. Insights gained in the learning phase are now used to turn transformation intent into clearer objectives and related transformational goals for teaching and learning. The group meets to discuss the path forward and decide on the following broad areas for action:

Increased Communication: Establish ongoing and regular communication networks and channels between teachers and parents, and teachers and administrators. Appoint/elect liaisons between the different groups and set regular meeting times for information sharing.

Online Teaching and Learning Modules: Work with the Information Technology department at the school district level to create user-friendly learning modules for onboarding parents and teachers that can be accessed asynchronously. Have a launch date to inform and walk users through the training. Offer participation incentives for individual and school level participation.

Adjust Curricular Expectations. At the school level, institute monthly meetings between teachers and the parent teachers association to gauge challenges and opportunities and increase responsiveness for curricular adjustments as needed.

Ultimately, Linda guides the group to create goals that are grounded in the specific data that emerged from cycle 1. She also fine-tunes the recommendations from the group to ensure that the established goals are SMART—specific, measurable, attainable, relevant, and time-bound (Doran, 1981).

Once the goals have been set, Linda and her assistants decide on the kinds of data that will be collected to assess whether projected changes have the desired outcomes. In this case, they will collect pre- and postplan implementation data from a subset of the school district population of principals, teachers, and parents. They also plan to make use of other available measures to get a more comprehensive view of the change effort—for example, student performance data, measures of student engagement as recorded by moments logged on, and other indices of student engagement and learning that might be applicable.

TAC Phase 2: Implementing

Linda and her leadership team work to implement the transformative application plan. In keeping with best practice for implementation, they follow key recommendations drawn from the literature. First, they create a written plan that details the specifics of achieving the goals in clear, simple language (Pfeffer & Sutton, 1999) and employ "if–then" logic, ("if we do this, then this will be enabled") as recommended to help them with imagining next steps (Grant, 2014; Wieber et al., 2012). Linda is mindful that the key to successful implementation is to maintain flexibility by regularly seeking feedback and being willing to adapt the proposed actions as needed (Zenger & Folkman, 2016). Therefore, along with the district level leadership team, she puts in place processes to collect and use feedback regularly to reshape the implementation. For example, she identifies a point person at each school in the district and schedules regular implementation updates with these school leaders. At the end of the implementation phase, data are collected according to plan.

TAC Phase 3: Evaluating

At the end of the transformative application cycle, the team evaluates whether set benchmarks were met. The data collected from TAC phase 2 are analyzed relative to stated transformational goals. Linda and the TAM leadership team prepare a report that clearly shows progress relative to stated goals and share this report with the school district administration and participants.

Given that change processes can extend over long periods of time, Linda and the TAM leadership team agree to conclude the active phase of the project with a summative report while recommended actions for improvement continue. To conclude the project, the team meets for a final focused discussion. Linda leads the discussion with key evaluation questions as follows:

- What was achieved and what was not?
- To what extent has the implementation produced effective change efforts?
- What adjustments can be made to existent plans?
- Will it be necessary to have a second round of the application cycle?

Based on the response to these questions, Linda and her team do the important work of auditing the project and creating a plan for next steps as needed or project completion and deliverables.

Linda invites the original team of participants and the TAM leadership team to a celebratory dinner. The purpose of this gathering is twofold. First, she thanks participants for their good work. Second, she uses this opportunity to revisit the transformational objectives that were targeted at the personal and group level. She engages the team in an informal discussion once again about how they have changed personally and as a group as they moved from transformational learning goals to transformative application goals.

Scenario # 2 Changing Course—Recalibrating for Leadership Development

The Empowered Women's Leadership Development Group has been in existence for 20 years. The group started under the dynamic leadership of a visionary leader who was intent on providing leadership development opportunities for women in various settings. The founding leaders have since left to follow other career pursuits.

When the group first began, its purpose and mission had been based on best leadership practices of the time. Now, research evidence and emerging models of effective leadership development have revealed more effective pathways for leadership development especially targeted at women. Two years after the leaders' departure, the new leadership team has begun to question their original views on women's leadership development. They realize that their perspectives are shifting. What if group members are also experiencing similar shifts in thinking? How might insights gained from a careful examination of their views on women's leadership development impact their self-leadership and also help them to reshape the group's mission and purpose?

The Transformative Learning Cycle: Changing Course

As the leadership team thinks about these questions, they agree to take proactive steps to think through their conceptions of leadership development and how that might help them reshape the mission and purpose of the Empowered Women's Leadership Development Group. They decide to apply the TAM model which they learned about at a recent leadership conference on this topic.

TLC Phase 1: Preparation

The group meets to plan a one-week TAM research retreat. The current president, Kayla, and her three group officers form the participant pool. They hold an initial meeting to determine the focus and scope of the TAM project. They make use of the TAM planning template. First, they set the research questions as follows:

1. What experiences/practices have been most critical in our leadership development?
2. How are our current leadership development experiences/practices consistent or inconsistent with the literature on leadership development for women?

They also set the broad twofold study objectives as follows:

1. To understand the best experiences/practices for leadership development of women at the nexus of personal experiences and relevant literature.
2. To utilize perspective taking and group knowledge about leadership development of women at the nexus of personal experiences and relevant literature to reposition self-leadership and to chart a new course for the Empowered Women's Leadership Development Group.

The team then decides on the logistics around the event and selects relevant reading resources. They estimate a time frame post retreat of about six months to work through the transformative application cycle. As part of the preparation process, each woman also writes a two-page response to the following writing prompt: *What in my view are best practices for leadership development of women?* They also send out an open-ended satisfaction survey to all group members to assess the extent to which members perceive that the Empowered Women's Leadership Development Group is effectively meeting their leadership needs and to seek input on targeted areas for improvement. They agree that this survey will provide good baseline data for the TAM project. They ask a staff member to input and analyze the data so that they can look at it at the end of the transformative learning cycle.

TLC Step 2: Exploration

Given the retreat setting, the group adopts set times for writing exploration and related activities as follows:

Day 1. On the first day, President Kayla opens the first session with a broad overview of what will happen over the next few days. She then introduces the topic with a selected documentary on the leadership experiences of a prominent leader and talks about her own leadership development journey. In the first exploration activity, participants write a reflective response to a writing prompt. Kayla reminds everyone about what they learned about autoethnographic writing. They should elaborate on points with detailed examples, and/or references to literature, and they should aim to be as honest as possible. The group makes use of an online learning platform to share their work. The women separate for the independent writing exercise in response to the prompt:

> Reflecting on my earliest experiences with leadership to now, which incidents emerge as most critical to my leadership development? What made these incidents so critical?

In the afternoon, the group reconvenes for sharing. First, they discuss and review qualitative interviewing techniques in preparation for the next steps in data exploration. Then they divide into pairs and exchange writings for peer reading and commenting. After the reading sessions, pairs take the afternoon period to meet in a cozy spot with light refreshments and take turns asking each other questions about what they had written.

Day 2. In the morning, the group engages in some opening preliminary exercises. However, the major task is for pairs to work together to arrive at four to five common and/or dissimilar themes in their responses. In the afternoon session, pairs reconnect, review their collated list of themes and work to reduce the combined list to about six to eight points of agreement.

Day 3. These initial explorations have given rise to new questions and subquestions. Therefore, they decide to repeat another round of exploration on the third day using these new questions and following the same model outlined for the first two days.

Day 4. The group gathers to listen to a presentation on leadership models that President Kayla has prepared from the material they have all read. After the presentation, they engage in a focus group discussion in which they look for synergies between their discoveries and the literature. In the last step of exploration, each of the women write a reflection paper on how, if in any way, their thinking has changed through the exploration process. These responses are also added to the data pool.

TLC Phase 3: Discovery

In this project, exploration and discovery flow seamlessly together. However, once the point of saturation is reached with data collection and reflection papers turned in, the focus turns fully to the discovery phase.

Day 5. The group engages in a holistic examination of the data to understand what was learned from the topic and to further negotiate meaning. They focus on the transformation experienced at three levels.

- **Personal Level:** They reflect on what they learned in response to the research question and compare their pre-retreat response to their final reflection paper.
- **Group Level:** At the group level, they examine what was learned and how the group changed through the critical dialogic process of meaning making, multivocality and working across differences.
- **Community Level:** As a culminating point to the first cycle of the TAM process, they then focus on how their shared experiences and discoveries might be used to guide and reposition the organization to more effectively serve the Empowered Women's Leadership Group.

Before moving on to the next cycle, they also look at the results from the satisfaction survey to see if and how their findings are consistent or inconsistent with responses from group members.

The Transformative Application Cycle: Changing Course

At the end of the transformative learning cycle, the TAM project team meets to reflect on what was learned in the first cycle. In particular, looking at the data first from a personal lens and then from an organizational leadership lens, they begin to think through next steps in their personal leadership development and the missional direction of the Empowered Women's Leadership Development Group.

TAC Phase 1: Planning

The team revises the initial working transformational objective and moves towards measurable goals.

Day 6. They operationalize objectives into SMART goals with clear benchmarks around broad areas targeted at the personal and organizational levels. At the personal level, the women agree on the following:

- Revise/create personal leadership mission and vision to reflect insights gained from the TAM exploration.
- Align personal leadership development practices with newer theoretical models and best practices for women's leadership development.
- Provide accountability and support for each other to keep abreast of advances in leadership development.
- Create a workshop and/or presentation to demonstrate how other women can engage in the TAM process for ongoing professional development.

As they discuss next steps for their personal leadership development, the women realize they have benefited so much from the experience that they would like to form a group to provide ongoing support and accountability for each other in line with their leadership goals. They hope to make this retreat experience an annual event and to plan regular meetups during the year. At the organization level, they identify the following broad areas for transformation:

- Revise organizational mission and vision to reflect theoretical advances and best practices in women's leadership development.
- Provide training around diversity, equity, and belonging.
- Provide ongoing training opportunities in the use of technology.
- Create more opportunities for sponsorship and mentorship among members.
- Foster the development of communities of practice and mastermind groups.

They select a leader to oversee implementation of the plan. The team decides to recruit volunteers from the membership group to help with the implementation and evaluation processes that will follow.

Day 7. The women end the retreat session with a celebratory sightseeing tour and evening dinner to culminate their time together.

TAC Phase 2: Implementing

On the way home, the women coordinate calendars and begin planning for the year ahead. They set a monthly meeting time for the third Friday of each month. At the organizational level, the implementation group works on the project goals. The implementation director provides the leadership group with progress updates. Set times are established for bimonthly or monthly meetings to monitor progress and make adjustments as needed to ensure expected outcomes. After the implementation plans have been in place for an agreed six months, all members of the Empowered Women's Leadership Group are invited to complete the original satisfaction survey again.

TAC Phase 3: Evaluating

The self-selected womens' leadership support group which emerged from the retreat continues to monitor and evaluate their leadership progress post retreat and beyond. The team also reviews the data collected at the end of the previous phase to see how well the action plan is working for the larger group. Based on their ongoing review and evaluation of these and other data, they continue to make adjustments as needed to achieve targeted organizational changes.

Scenario #3: Beyond the Book

Chris is a publisher who brings together teams of authors from around the world to create coauthored books. Authors work independently sending in their chapter drafts to him, which he then passes on to his publishing team. He is aware that in past coauthored books he has done, many authors were so intent on writing their own chapters that they did not fully benefit from the writings of the other authors. He would like to change this paradigm. Chris would also like to cultivate more of a community of authors who can continue to support and encourage each other long after the project is completed. Chris recently took a course in application of the TAM for individual and group transformation, and he wonders if this might just be the tool he needs to make this change possible.

The Transformative Learning Cycle: Beyond the Book

Chris decides to implement the TAM model on his current book project. This book will focus on strategies that minority employees are using in U.S. organizations to deal with racial stress and trauma. He is hopeful that the model that he will be creating for this community of authors will be a catalyst for the group to replicate support communities even after the book is published.

TLC Phase 1: Preparation

For this recruitment effort, Chris takes a different approach. In addition to putting together a call for authors to be a part of the coauthored book project around a common topic, he also includes additional benefits: (a) becoming part of a supportive learning community of authors; and (b) learning strategies for replicating support groups around the topic post production. Potential authors are made aware of the scope of the work and the time frame for commitment pre- and postpublication. Chris plans to kick off the event with a virtual launch party since he anticipates that authors will be from different geographic locations in the United States. In advance of the launch party, Chris enrolls individuals in a virtual learning platform which will become the repository for data. He decides to use a combination of concurrent and sequential data collection approaches: independent writing exercises, focus group discussions, and threaded discussions. He also settles on a group size of about 8–10 participants and a period of six months to work through the first iteration of the TAM.

Prior to the start of data collection, Chris recruits a volunteer to serve as a project assistant to help him lead and moderate the discussion forum in the virtual learning platform. The assistant creates a series of writing prompts to be launched and responded to in two-week cycles. The assistant also sets up discussion boards to complement the data collection.

As already noted, the purpose of this TAM project is embedded in the call for authors. In this case the project leader, Chris, sets the purpose and overarching question in advance of meeting with participants and makes them aware of these so they can determine if they want to be part of the project. He also sets the overarching research questions at the personal and communal level for each prospective author as follows:

1. What are my personal experiences of dealing with racial trauma as a minority individual within U.S. organizations?
2. What strategies have I used to help me deal with racial trauma experienced within U.S. organizations?
3. What commonalities/differences exist in the shared experiences of minority individuals experiencing and dealing with racial trauma within U.S. organizations?

Chris also sets the broad twofold study objectives for the study, targeted at understanding how individuals deal with racial trauma as minority individuals within organizations and the working transformational objectives for the TAM project as follows:

1. To understand the commonalities and differences in personal experiences of dealing with racial trauma as minority individuals within U.S. organizations.
2. To utilize perspective-taking and group knowledge to foster empathetic understanding among others about racial trauma experienced by minority individuals within U.S. organizations.
3. To lead and inspire coauthors to replicate communities of support for minority individuals in their respective contexts.

Chris also sets up a discovery call with each prospective author. In this call, he restates the scope and extent of the project to ensure that authors understand and are committed to the long-term goals of the project.

TLC Phase 2: Exploration

Data collection takes place in the virtual learning platform. Participants respond independently to set writing prompts, and they also participate in threaded discussions online. According to Chang et al. (2013), sequential data collecting presents a unique advantage over concurrent forms. In a threaded discussion, the ideas expressed by one person can spark ideas and thoughts from others. Hence, it can provide a different kind of rich data. In making use of both forms of data collection, Chris hopes to maximize the benefits of both approaches to yield deep insight into the selected topic.

TLC Phase 3: Discovery

Planning, exploration, and discovery flow together seamlessly in this project as a result of the nature and scope of the online activities. For example, data are taken during the application period, through concurrent and sequential data collection once the study begins, and collection is ongoing during the exploration phase as individuals collaboratively make meaning about their experiences through threaded discussion, assignments, and focus group sessions. The schedule is summarized in Table 6.1:

Table 6.1. TAM-CAE Example of a Schedule for the Transformative Learning Cycle (TLC)

Activity Type	Time	Instruction
Independent Writing	Part of the Application Process	Briefly respond to the following writing prompt(s):
		What story do you plan to share for your chapter on a triggering event in which you experienced racial trauma?
		What strategies have you used in the past or are using in the present for dealing with racial trauma as a minority individual within a U.S. organization?
		What commonalities do you think exist in how others like you are dealing with racial trauma as minority individuals within U.S. organizations?
Threaded Discussion Prompt	Prior to Launch Party	Introduce yourself to the rest of the team with an attached photo. Where do you live? What drew you to this project? Post a question to your peers. Respond to at least two other members.
Threaded Discussion Prompt	Prior to Launch Party	Describe in a short paragraph a defining moment in your experience of racial trauma within an organization and how you dealt with it.
		Post a question to your peers. Respond to at least two other members.
Virtual Meeting Launch Party	Day of Launch Party	Bring an item to the party that in some way is meaningful to you in relation to your choice of a defining moment of racial trauma or how you overcame it. Be prepared to share in small group breakout sessions why this is meaningful to you.
		Leader shares the template for the chapters in a brief webinar and invites participants to begin drafting stories with a set deadline for first drafts.

Activity Type	Time	Instruction
Threaded Discussion	Post Launch Party	What did you learn about each other's experiences of racial trauma based on what was shared in the breakout session?
		What commonalities/differences existed in your collective stories?
		Post a question to your peers. Respond to at least two other members.
Webinar	Writing the Chapters	The leader shares pertinent information on editing and revising first draft and peer content reviewing.
		The leader invites authors to review and revise drafts for peer content editing.
Sharing scripts Independent Reading and Meaning Making	Post Writing First Draft	Teams of about three to four authors exchange drafts for reading/inserting probing questions.
Subgroups Focus Group Meeting 1	Post Peer Editing	Smaller subgroups meet to review drafts and to probe in focus group sessions. Sessions are recorded as part of the data collection process.
		Following the focus group meeting, authors are tasked to independently come up with five to seven common/divergent themes in their collective stories based on the preliminary data.
		Authors return to editing and revising their drafts and submit final draft before Subgroup Meeting 2
Subgroups Focus Group Meeting 2	Post Peer Editing	Teams meet to reflect on each other's stories, review each other's themes and negotiate a final set of themes, about five to seven, for their subgroup.
Whole Group Meeting	Post Independent Group Meetings	All subgroups discuss themes and the entire group led by the project leader negotiates the final lessons and project takeaways.
Independent Reflection	Post Whole Group Meeting	Participants return to their entry essays and reflect on how their response to the question and how their thoughts were confirmed/disconfirmed.
		They also reflect on how if in any way this group process has changed them.
Final Webinar	Whole Group	The leader provides a framework for post-book accountability and support for the community of authors.
		The project leader shares a customized model for how authors can begin and lead a support community for minority individuals in organizations.
		The transformative learning cycle concludes with a celebratory send off and a memento is given to authors to now become part of the post-publication support community.

The Transformative Application Cycle: Support Beyond the Book

In the process of being part of this online learning community employing the TAM, individuals benefit from the support and solidarity that are embedded in the autoethnographic process. Not only do they gain personal insight into the topic, they are also able to see linkages between their experiences and those of others in the group. They have formed a community that is well positioned to move from learning to action. The group of authors now meets with Chris to finalize transformational learning objectives beyond book completion.

TAC Phase 1: Planning

Chris invites the entire group to become part of the action plan for creating, a model to nurture communities of practice that support individuals serving in institutions where they represent the minority group. The group agrees on set guidelines for operating beyond the book. They set regular accountability meetings as well as SMART goals and timelines. Chris shares the plan for replication of the model/s to create other communities of practice. Together, the group comes up with three possible models that can be used based on preference. These are as follows:

- **TAM Explorations:** Teams can embark on an exploration of racial trauma or a selected topic within their organizational context. Instead of completing a coauthored book project, the purpose would be to disseminate collected information through conference presentations, reports, and/or journal articles. Through the process of employing the TAM, teams can also target personal, group, and organizational transformations as intended outcomes of such explorations.
- **Reading Circles:** Teams can form a reading circle using the published book to stimulate group discussion and reflection. These meetings may provide additional data points and strategies that can be added to the growing content on strategies for dealing with racial trauma in organizations.
- **Working Across Differences:** Teams can decide to work across differences and invite diverse participants to create a group in which they write and respond to a triggering racial/ethnic or other event written from their differing perspectives. Using elements of autoethnographic work that include perspective taking, engaging in critical dialogues, and group meaning making, they can work to facilitate deeper understanding for the other.

As a result of this meeting, six of the authors commit to starting a group of their own, and the remaining authors commit to assisting self-selected leaders through the process. Chris works with leaders to operationalize group goals, specify steps in the replication processes and timelines, and set and select evaluation metrics for each group. He also encourages teams to build celebration into the group process to foster ongoing community building and buy-in.

TAC Phase 2: Implementing

Beyond the book completion, Chris meets with group leaders based on an agreed schedule. These meetings provide important information for readjusting the various models and brainstorming for potentially scaling up to create a membership community with possibilities for professional development, conferences, and possible meetups.

TAC Phase 3: Evaluating

Chris and his team of leaders have set up a system of ongoing evaluation for the project. Under Chris's leadership, teams engage in initial intake data collection, mid-cycle formative assessment, and end-cycle data collection relevant to program outcomes. They utilize a complement of self-report assessment measures and qualitative measures to assess communal support experiences and the other benefits. Teams also make use of other indices to assess program reach and effectiveness: for example, number of meetings held; number of subgroups; number of members in groups; deliverables from groups including papers presented, articles written, and workshops conducted. Chris and the leadership team discuss and make use of these data to continue to adjust program offerings as needed.

The TAM in the Real World

The three hypothetical scenarios presented in this chapter have been selected to match a variety of situations that are likely to present themselves in organizations in which a collaborative approach to solution generation is best. In each case, we have imaginatively fleshed out an idealized pathway from program start to completion. As in the previous chapter, we have done so mainly as a pedagogical device to show examples of what is possible. At the same time, we encourage users of the TAM model to think creatively about how to approach each of the cycles and phases to best match their needs while attending to methodological considerations.

The scenarios presented here illustrate two aspects of the model. First, they show its utility for use in a variety of probable situations for which change solutions are needed. Secondly, they show that there is much room for creativity and flexibility throughout the TAM process for teams to customize the TAM to meet their change effort objectives. These two factors make the TAM a suitable choice for desired change efforts in multiple contexts.

Summary

There is something special that happens when individuals gather in community and choose to become open and vulnerable about issues that are of mutual concern. Inasmuch as cognitive understanding and interrogation of the hows and whys of issues are useful first steps in working towards solutions, beyond understanding, we are often in search of tangible and practical next steps. Working in community using a collaborative autoethnographic approach to applying the TAM offers a workable approach to achieving this objective. What is unique about the TAM applied to collaborative inquiry is that it offers two important benefits. It provides opportunities for individuals to pool their collective experiences to gain a better understanding of an issue, and it also fosters perspective taking so that we can come to understand each other better. Through communal sharing, the community benefits from the rich diversity of thoughts and insights, begins to see the issue from a multifocal frame of reference, and can begin the collective effort of working towards a common solution. In the process of doing this head and heart work, individuals inevitably find that they themselves are changed, and they are now well positioned to be change agents in the contexts in which they find themselves.

References

Bieri, F., Tolstikov-Mast, Y. Gambrell, K., Goerman, P., Hernandez, K. C., Krause, W., Mneimneh, Z. N., & Walker, J. L. (2022). Success in International Leadership Research. In Y. Tolstikov-Mast,

F. Bieri, & J. L.Walker (Eds.), *Handbook of International and Cross-Cultural Leadership Research Processes: Perspectives, Practice, Instruction* (pp. 587–602). Taylor and Francis.

Braun, V., & Clarke, V. (2006). Using thematic analysis in psychology. *Qualitative Research in Psychology, 3*(2), 77–101. https://doi.org/10.1191/1478088706qp063oa

Bryman, A. (2015). *Social research methods.* Oxford University Press.

Chang, H. (2008). *Autoethnography as method.* Routledge.

Chang, H., Ngunjiri, F. W., & Hernandez, K. C. (2013). *Collaborative autoethnography.* Routledge.

Doran, G. T. (1981). There's a SMART way to write management's goals and objectives. *Management Review, 70*(11), 35–36.

Grant, H. (2014). Get your team to do what it says it's going to do. *Harvard Business Review, 92*(5), 82–87.

Hernandez, K. C., & Longman, K. A. (2020). Changing the face of leadership in higher education: "Sponsorship" as a strategy to prepare emerging leaders of color. *Journal of Ethnographic and Qualitative Research, 15*(2), 117–136.

Hernandez, K. C., & Ngunjiri, F. W. (2013). Relationships and communities. In T. E. Adams, C. Ellis, & S. Holman Jones (Eds.), *Handbook of autoethnography* (pp. 262–280). Left Coast Press.

Pfeffer, J., & Sutton, R. I. (1999). The smart-talk trap. *Harvard Business Review, 77*(3), 134–142.

Wieber, F., Thürmer, J. L., & Gollwitzer, P. M. (2012). Collective action control by goals and plans: Applying a self-regulation perspective to group performance. *American Journal of Psychology, 125*(3), 275–290. https://doi.org/10.5406/amerjpsyc.125.3.0275

Zenger, J., & Folkman, J. (2016, May 23). *4 ways to be more effective at execution.* Harvard Business Review. https://hbr.org/2016/05/4-ways-to-be-more-effective-at-execution

SEVEN

TAM and Future Directions

Our Story

Heewon: Kathy-Ann, would you be interested in working with me to write an autoethnographic book for practitioners?

Kathy-Ann: Hmmm . . . Wow! Sounds like a great idea. I know we have been talking about the need for such a book for a while now. Hmmmm, I am not sure I want to commit to another book project. I just have too much going on.

Heewon: Yeah, I am overwhelmed too. Not even sure I have the time. However, I think this book is so needed.

Kathy-Ann: I agree. The transformative impact of autoethnographic work has come up again and again in my own work, yet it is generally not the primary objective of the work I am doing.

Heewon: Exactly! This could be a way for us to show the path for making transformation the primary intent.

Kathy-Ann: You know, I like the idea, but the workload of writing another book. (Sigh). I don't think I can handle it right now.

Heewon: Well, we could find another author to work with us so the workload would not be too much for any one of us.

Kathy-Ann: Hmm, that's not a bad idea. Do you have someone in mind?

Heewon: Yes. What about asking Wendy? I will reach out to her.

****

Heewon: Hi Wendy, would you be interested in coauthoring a book with Kathy-Ann and me on transformative autoethnography for practitioners?

Wendy: Hmm . . . That sounds interesting. Tell me more.

****

WE (KATHY-ANN AND HEEWON) BEGAN our work in autoethnography many years ago. Since then, our coauthored (along with Faith Ngunjiri) book on the topic, *Collaborative Auteothnography* (2013) thrust our work into the spotlight and provided multiple opportunities to teach the method and embark on our own scholarship. In all of our past projects conducted up to that point, we had seen firsthand the transformative element that kept emerging in our work, sometimes even almost upstaging the primary purpose of a given study. At the same time, Wendy, who had done her autoethnographic dissertation under the chairship of Heewon, had also emerged from her dissertation journey changed in unanticipated ways. The common thread that ran through our experiences was the growing recognition of the transformative aspect of autoethnographic work and an increasing desire to advocate for the centering of transformation in autoethnographic inquiry.

Even so, none of us was prepared to take on the job of writing a book about this, especially during a global pandemic. It was just not an opportunity we looked for, but once we thought about it some more, the decision was clear. How could we not? Our evolving identities as scholars and practitioners—with increasingly stronger leanings towards the practitioner end of the continuum—made the decision easier. We (Kathy-Ann and Heewon), had transitioned from our early career positioning in education to organizational leadership and leadership development. The interdisciplinary nature of the field and our program focus on the scholar/activist model were working to shift our mindset as well to think more intentionally about the change efforts that were needed to do leadership well in academic, business, and nonprofit contexts. Wendy was also drawn to the autoethnographic approach. It resonated with her professional social work training and her desire to choose a methodology that would fulfill the important social function of giving space to the voices of the marginalized toward the purpose of social change. The clear connections between autoethnography and some of the therapeutic and healing functions of her profession expanded her commitment to using this methodology in even more practice settings. More importantly however, having engaged in and immersed ourselves in autoethnographic inquiry over many years, we had also changed. Autoethnography had become an extension of how we lived and worked. These experiences convinced us that this book was timely and needed.

Transformative Autoethnography

Autoethnography situates inquirers in a liminal space of advancing scholarship while simultaneously affecting practice. As we have argued in this book, this is a unique space with tremendous opportunities for benefits to both scholars and practitioners. We grounded our discussion in the transformative approaches of great thinkers such as Kuhn (1962), Freire (1970), and Habermas (1984), and later works by Mezirow (1997; 2000). Such transformative approaches have historically sought to disrupt the power hierarchies in our world, the academy, the corporate world, and the political and social spheres.

Since its emergence on the scene as a novel approach to investigating social phenomena, autoethnography has continued to evolve to meet the needs of inquirers and the zeitgeist of the times. In particular, we see a growing focus on the pragmatics of inquiry. How can we do something that works to affect intended outcomes? The benefit of autoethnography is that it offers a both/and solution for the needs of social inquiry. If done well, it can simultaneously address the need for understanding a problem or issue and facilitate needed change through the storying processes and product.

The personal story is at the heart of autoethnographic inquiry. Stories are the links in the transformation chain process because there is something unique that happens to us through storytelling. The stories of autoethnographers have the capacity to move listeners in personally meaningful ways. For some, the connection may feel like a religious experience, perhaps like sitting in a pew listening to the testimony of a fellow faith traveler. Or it may be like an encounter in a support group, where one senses a common experience with the person sharing their struggle with alcohol, death, or divorce (Grant, 2010; Lengelle, 2021; Nicholas, 2016). The connection made through autoethnographic work might leave the listener stunned, surprised, even with a rapid heartbeat. Others may experience an internal shift, similar to what may happen when viewing a Picasso painting, listening to a Handel aria, or hearing the poetry of Emily Dickinson; in the process of listening or entering into the autoethnographer's shared experience, a connection is made between them and other, and like art, it speaks transformatively (Leavy, 2020b). In this way, autoethnography owes much of its transformative capabilities to the power of story, and the magic of artful telling. There is a different impact between sharing information and sharing experiences; mental information does not land in the whole self the way someone's graphic experiences might be "felt."

In this book we have focused on autoethnography as a key addition to a growing repertoire of transformative rather than primarily informative inquiry practices. Autoethnography straddles the line between inquiry and transformative practice through its strong focus on storytelling as a critical link in the transformation chain. To this end, we see autoethnography continuing to evolve beyond even what we have discussed in this book. Autoethnography can continue to impact our lives through the transformative power of story.

Journey to the TAM

We wrote this book during various states of isolation as the COVID-19 global pandemic continued on. For much of the time, we watched as life as we had known it for our entire life up to that point, began to change all around us. The widespread adoption of digital technology, video conferencing, and other forms of virtual communications made it possible to conduct business, social interactions, religious attendance, and even education in new ways. These changes in how we live and communicate continue to shape our thinking and approach to life for the twenty-first century and beyond. We have been able to envision new ways of doing things to achieve expected outcomes.

This capacity for adaptability that has become a potent and very visible force in our day-to-day lives since COVID-19 shows little signs of abating. In fact, as we have thought about it, we are excited by this adaptability in the sociopolitical context and the potential possibilities for social inquiry methods like autoethnography. We envision a continuing evolution of autoethnographic explorations: to continue to shape our scholarship and practice; to impact our personal lives, the way we live, and how we relate to those within our ecological contexts; and to impact our professional lives, the way we work and conduct business in a fast changing digital landscape.

Our Scholarship and Practice

Autoethnographic scholarship continues to push the boundaries of what is considered research in critical ways. Since autoethnography began many years ago, we now see the proliferation of journals specifically focused on this genre of writing. Once viewed as mere navel gazing, autoethnography is now securely occupying its rightful place as legitimate research practice. In one pivotal step in that direction, the American Educational Research Association, the premier U.S. professional organization for educational research, presented a landmark article in 2012 entitled *Translating Autoethnography Across the AERA Standards: Toward Understanding Autoethnographic Scholarship as Empirical Research* (Hughes et al., 2012). This article provided a much-needed framework for researchers to advance scholarship with clear criteria for how it would be assessed and valued. In 2013, the team of Holman Jones, Adams, and Ellis published *The Handbook of Autoethnography*, an excellent reference for researchers intent on advancing autoethnographic inquiry. Eight years later, the authors released a new and updated edition of the same (Adams, Holman Jones, & Ellis, 2021). These resources provide valuable additions to the field and necessary know-how for inquirers. They also continue to extend the conversation about the continuing evolution of autoethnographic practice.

At the same time, the increasing ubiquity of digital technologies raises questions about what inquiry will look like in digital space. What technological tools will be available to us for the future? What kinds of questions will arise about relationships within the nascent contexts of the digital world? What methodological considerations will they bring to the forefront of inquiry? Without a doubt such changes will impact our relational connections, the kinds of stories we tell, and how we tell them in virtual space. There are more options available to us for inquiry of the self that uses a variety of modalities for collecting, analyzing and even presenting our work using a variety of modalities. Social media and the ever-expanding possibilities through virtual meeting spaces have widened the reach and impact of autoethnographic works particularly during the COVID-19 pandemic. For example, in the summer of 2021 Marlen Harrison launched a fully digital magazine, *The AutoEthnographer*, "dedicated to presenting the creative side of autoethnography" (Harrison, 2021). Two Facebook groups, Critical Autoethnography and IAANI (International Association for Autoethnography and Narrative Practice), became the main news-sharing hubs for virtual events featuring autoethnography throughout the COVID-19 pandemic. These virtual events were perfect platforms for the growing global community of autoethnographers to gather, share their work, and develop an interest in autoethnographic inquiry.

The field has also continued to see more and more articles published highlighting the transformative element in autoethnographic work. We position this book as an extension of those conversations and an addition to the body of methodological frameworks for social inquiry. We also situate this work in the liminal space between scholarship at practice, reflecting our own journey towards the praxis end of the research continuum, and as an offering to inquirers who live primarily in the world of praxis. Even as recent events in our world have shifted with an unavoidable focus on what works, the TAM advanced in this book is a tool for scholars and practitioners moving along this continuum to effect changes through the process and products of their inquiry.

Living an Autoethnographic Life

For those committed to autoethnographic work, the intimacy of this line of social inquiry often becomes an inextricable extension of themselves. Even though social science research has often sought to separate the self from scholarship in a nod to positivist approaches to social science research, much of the work that we do as scholars and practitioners emanates from our personal experiences (Ngunjiri et al., 2010). Autoethnographic work allows us to situate ourselves in our work unapologetically and to address sensitive issues with microscopic accuracy. These up close and personal views of ourselves as individuals in relational spaces change us and by extension those around us—our work becomes a dynamic and living part of our experiences.

It is not surprising therefore that Holman Jones (2018) asked, "What does it mean to live an autoethnographic life?" (p. 539) and, further, is an autoethnographic life synonymous with a life of transformative intent, an activist life? Given our clear focus in this book, we argue that autoethnography is at its core transformative. In that respect, the answer would be "yes." Autoethnography is an "activist activity" and those who engage in it are activists (Holman Jones, 2018, p. 539). The transformative intent that is inherent in autoethnographic work makes those who choose to engage in it active change agents.

Additionally, the capacity of autoethnography to blur the art/science divide also allows for the therapeutic benefits of art to the human spirit. Bochner and Adams (2020) described autoethnography as an artful science, able to disrupt the unhelpful binaries of sometimes limiting traditional methodologies. In particular, the artistic element holds potential for self care and healing. Patricia Leavy (2020b) an arts-based researcher, has observed that "the arts invite empathetic participation . . . art as a cultural intervention. It's a means of putting other stories, images, or perspectives into the culture. It's a means of getting people to think and feel differently." Altogether, autoethnography changes the inquirer and those who become recipients of the products of such inquiries.

Autoethnographic practice is life-shaping and life-changing, affecting us personally and those with whom we are connected. The autoethnographic experience invites the researcher to incorporate their whole selves into their inquiry as personal change agents and to extend an open invitation to others to be part of a transformative life experience.

Our Professional Lives

There is a persistent need for research in professional spaces to improve practice. Traditional social inquiry models have placed the capacity for research outside the purview of practitioners. The assumption is that objectivity and distancing are premier qualities for rigorous research. In line with normative valuing of more positivistic designs, companies often hire outside consultants and experts to come in to collect data, analyze and interpret it, present findings, and make recommendations for action. The TAM subverts this paradigm. While it is indeed necessary to have methodological expertise to conduct this kind of inquiry, this book and the additional reference resources cited here put the possibilities for inquiry in the hands of professionals who are insiders to the phenomenon under inquiry. This insider perspective provides a critical and unique vantage point for such investigations.

There are also additional benefits to be gained by those who are most invested in the topic when they are allowed to chart a course from inquiry to problem solution. First, the level of scrutiny and insider knowledge that lies within those who are insiders to the problem/issue at hand allows for a deeper and richer level of inquiry. They occupy a front row seat to explore issues with a great depth of understanding. Second, there is the inherent buy-in and a sense of ownership that allows participants in this line of inquiry to take responsibility for outcomes personally. Third, given the strong relational focus of both individual and collaborative approaches to autoethnography, individuals who embark on such explorations are able to form strong relational bonds with far reaching impacts for team work, organizational culture, and feelings of overall work satisfaction. Finally, this approach to inquiry is based on a levelling of hierarchical power structures within organizations with tremendous potential for humanizing and bridging divides between supervisor and supervisees, administration and staff members, and between others of similarities and others of difference, thus allowing for a professional space in which we are bonded together to accomplish similar goals while acknowledging and being sensitive to each other's humanity. In our view, the potential for these relational benefits from applications of the TAM bodes well for the future of working relationships within professional spaces.

Conclusion

Our intent in writing this book has been to make a clearer path for doing transformative work through autoethnography. The capacity to effect change in individuals through the process and products of autoethnographic inquiry has been well established in the literature, yet the way of bringing the transformative intent to center stage has not been well captured to date. In that respect, our work builds on the scholarship of many others, extending the conversation about how best to apprehend the inherent benefits of autoethnographic work. But more than just adding to the discussion, our intent has been to provide a clear and accessible pathway for practitioners to move from inquiry methods to transformative outcomes. The TAM delivers on that intent.

With all of that said, however, we acknowledge that the transformative benefits of the TAM, while potentially accessible to those who use it, are not guaranteed. In the realm of social science research, we are not able to effect outcomes with the precision of mathematical transformations. Change often happens incrementally. It is more likely to be subtle rather than drastic. As such, if we are not vigilant we might miss seeing change effects altogether as we painstakingly work through the TAM cycles and phases. In particular, in cases where we attempt to use the TAM to bridge divides among others of difference, the work will challenge us. It may even be confrontational, and might seem never-ending. At times, it may appear that all we have done is to dialogue ad nauseum with no clear points of agreement. However, to leave a TAM inquiry with this perception will be analogous to "missing the forest for the trees." In working through the cycles of transformative learning and application with the attendant phases, transformation happens. Autoethnographers learn to see self not only from their own eyes in new ways, but from the eyes of others, to come under the gaze of strangers, and to be ready for the surprise and challenge that comes with new discoveries about self, others, and society. Transformation is present in the process, products, and people who have courageously embarked on provoking change through transformative autoethnographic practice.

References

Adams, T. E., Holman Jones, S., & Ellis, C. (Eds.) (2021). *Handbook of autoethnography* (2nd ed.). Routledge.

Bochner, A. P., & Adams, T. E. (2020). Autoethnography as applied communication research. In D. O'Hair & M. J. O'Hair (Eds.), *The Handbook of Applied Communication Research* (pp. 707–729). John Wiley & Sons.

Chang, H., Ngunjiri, F. W., & Hernandez, K. C. (2013). *Collaborative autoethnography*. Routledge.

Freire, P. (1970). *Pedagogy of the oppressed*. Herter and Herter.

Grant, A. (2010). Writing the reflexive self: An autoethnography of alcoholism and the impact of psychotherapy culture. *Journal of Psychiatric and Mental Health Nursing, 17*(7), 577–582. https://doi.org/10.1111/j.1365-2850.2010.01566.x

Habermas, J. (1984). *The theory of communicative action. Vol. 1: Reason and the rationalization of society* (T. McCarthy, Trans.). Beacon.

Harrison, M. (2021). The birth of an idea: Why I started *The AutoEthnographer*. https://theauto ethnographer.com/the-birth-of-an-idea/

Hughes, S., Pennington, J. L., & Makris, S. (2012). Translating autoethnography across the AERA standards: Toward understanding autoethnographic scholarship as empirical research. *Educational Researcher, 41*(6), 209–219. http://www.jstor.org/stable/23254131

Holman Jones, S. (2018). Creative selves/creative cultures: Critical autoethnography, performance, and pedagogy. In *Creative selves/creative cultures* (pp. 3–20). Palgrave Macmillan, Cham.

Holman Jones, S., Adams, T. E., & Ellis, C. (2013). *The handbook of autoethnography*. Routledge.

Kuhn, T. (1962). *The structure of scientific revolutions*. University of Chicago Press.

Leavy, P. (2020a). *Method meets art: Arts-based research practice* (3rd ed.). Guilford Publications.

Leavy, P. (2020b). Our brains and souls on art: An interview with Patricia Leavy. https://the sociologicalreview.org/collections/sociological-literature/our-brains-and-souls-on-art-u-melissa-anyiwo-interviews-patricia-leavy/

Lengelle, R. (2021). *Writing the self in bereavement: A story of love, spousal loss, and resilience*. Routledge.

Mezirow, J. (1997). Transformative learning: Theory to practice. In P. Cranton (Ed.), *Transformative learning in action: Insights from practice* (New Directions for Adult and Continuing Education (pp. 5–12). Jossey-Bass.

Mezirow, J. (2000). *Learning as transformation: Critical perspectives on a theory in progress.* Jossey-Bass.

Nicholas, G. (2016). "D" Is for divorce: An autoethnography. *Journal of Divorce & Remarriage, 57*(8), 586–591. https://doi.org/10.1080/10502556.2016.1233786

Ngunjiri, F. W., Hernandez, K. C., & Chang, H. (2010). Living autoethnography: Connecting life and research. *Journal of Research Practice, 6*(1), E1–E1.

About the Authors

Kathy-Ann C. Hernandez, Ph.D., is a professor of leadership in the College of Business and Leadership and cochair of the Ph.D. Program in Organizational Leadership at Eastern University in Pennsylvania. Dr. Hernandez is also CEO of Nexe Consulting in Philadelphia and consults with school districts, churches, schools, government offices, and colleges and universities nationally and internationally. She is a scholar/activist who has collaborated to conceptualize, secure funding, implement, manage, and evaluate several university-community partnership programs. In recognition of her work, she was awarded the Marlene Smigel Korn Humanitarian Award for excellent contribution in teaching, scholarship and/or service from the College of Education at Temple University.

Dr. Hernandez is a trained research methodologist who is actively involved in conducting research, facilitating research workshops, and teaching and advising on social science research methods and program evaluation. She has authored several book chapters and articles and serves as a coeditor for the *International Journal of Multicultural Education*. She is the coauthor of *Collaborative Autoethnography* (2013), with Heewon Chang and Faith Wambura Ngunjiri, as well as the author/presenter on several other autoethnographic-related scholarship projects. Her work has appeared in the *Handbook of Autoethnography, The International Journal of Qualitative Studies in Education*, and *The Journal of Research Practice*.

Her career mission is to bridge the gap between scholarship and practice through the sound application of research findings to solving real world problems. To this end, her research is focused on the salience of race/ethnicity, gender, spirituality, and social context in identity formation, leadership development, and social and academic outcomes for marginalized populations. She is also committed to interrogating and fostering the leadership development experiences of women and minorities in academic and public settings.

Heewon Chang, PhD, is a professor and chair of the PhD in Organizational Leadership program at Eastern University, located in St. Davids, Pennsylvania, USA. Over 30 years in higher education, she has maintained her triple identity of educator-scholar-mentor.

As an educator, her college teaching began with a graduate course in educational anthropology. Since then, she has taught undergraduate, master's, and PhD students. Her teaching areas have also expanded from educational anthropology to organizational leadership. During this expansion and change, she has maintained her love for qualitative research, diversity and multiculturalism, equity and justice, and global and cultural matters. She currently teaches Ph.D. courses with a focus on qualitative research, educational leadership, diversity and justice, and organizational culture.

As a scholar, she has published four books: *Adolescent Life and Ethos* (1992), *Autoethnography as Method* (2008), *Spirituality in Higher Education* (2011, coedited with Drick Boyd), and *Collaborative Autoethnography* (2013, coauthored Faith W. Ngunjiri and Kathy-Ann C. Hernandez). The last three books focus on autoethnography. Some of her journal articles and book chapters, focusing on autoethnography, appeared in *Qualitative Health Research* (2016), *Journal of Autoethnography* (2020), *Handbook of Autoethnography* (2013; 2022), and *Handbook of Sociological Ethnography* (2022).

Besides teaching and publishing her work, she enjoys providing scholarly mentoring to students through thesis or dissertation advising and to fellow scholars through journal editing. More recently, she assisted more than 20 PhD students to complete their dissertation journey. In addition, she served more than a thousand authors from various global contexts during the 20 years of service as the founding editor-in-chief of two academic journals, including the *International Journal of Multicultural Education*. She wrote about her experience as an editor in an autoethnographic essay: https://doi.org/10.18251/ijme.v20i3.1846.

Wendy A. Bilgen, PhD, LISW-S is an independent scholar, licensed therapist, and online adjunct instructor for Cornerstone University, Professional and Graduate Studies (PGS). She maintains a private counseling and leadership consulting practice in Antalya, Turkey, where she currently lives. Her PhD in Organizational Leadership is from Eastern University, USA. Her dissertation, *Constructing a Social Justice Leadership Identity: An Autoethnography of a Female Jewish Christian Social Worker Living in Turkey* began her ongoing research interest in autoethnography and critical research practices that lead toward individual and social transformation.

Over the last 30 years her professional and research interests have aligned with her life purpose exploring and developing narrative practices through diverse forms of inquiry. Exploring stories and experiences at the intersection of identity, culture, and spirituality focus her activities as an edge-walking practitioner, dividing time between teaching, counseling, speaking, research, and writing in the United States and Turkey. She continues to be drawn to trauma-informed research and practice and sees autoethnography as an integrating and innovative mode of engagement that is meaningful, healing, creative, practical, accessible, and transformative, all of which she hopes to bring into her interdisciplinary work as educator, therapist, and social worker.

Through her work she hopes that voices normally held at the margins of society would be stimulated to speak new wisdom and knowledge into all levels of society in order to stimulate social innovation and healing in individuals, organizations, communities, and societies around the globe.

Index